JEAN CHOI

FOUNDER OF WHAT GREAT GRANDMA ATE

KOREAN PALEO

80 BOLD-FLAVORED, GLUTEN-
AND GRAIN-FREE RECIPES

PAGE STREET
PUBLISHING CO.

PAGE STREET
PUBLISHING CO.

First published in 2018 by

Page Street Publishing Co.

27 Congress Street, Suite 105

Salem, MA 01970

www.pagestreetpublishing.com

Distributed by Macmillan, sales in Canada by The Canadian Manda Group.

22   21 20   19   18   1   2   3   4   5

ISBN-13: 978-1624146336

ISBN-10: 1624146333

Library of Congress Control Number: 2018943553

Cover and book design by Laura Gallant for Page Street Publishing Co.

Photography by Jean Choi

Illustration: istock/fatumwr

Printed and bound in Asia

To Umma and Appa, my amazing parents, who never let me for one second forget the beautiful country I came from and always spoke Korean to me at home. Thank you for giving me the invaluable gift of being bilingual and bicultural, so I can introduce our most beloved traditional dishes and customs to other families and cultures.

Saranghae!

CONTENTS

INTRODUCTION

I moved to a small town in New Jersey straight from Seoul, South Korea when I was seven years old without knowing a word of English, except maybe "hi" and "okay." Attending a brand new school full of kids and teachers who I couldn't understand was a huge culture shock for me, and the same goes for the food. I think it took me about two full years to actually enjoy American food enough that my mom didn't have to pack me strange Korean lunches that always raised the curiosity of my classmates.

It wasn't just that I didn't like American food. I resented the fact that I was forced to eat it as my mom started venturing more into cooking Western dishes, which my older brother somehow embraced immediately (way to be on my side, dude). My entire family still remembers the day my mom cooked pasta for dinner, and stubborn me refused to eat it. She, of course, patiently told me that this was dinner and there was nothing else to eat, and I broke out into a full-on screaming, bawling mess and stormed out of our townhouse, slamming the door behind me and everything. I think she gave me about thirty minutes to cry it out before coming out to drag me back inside.

So, needless to say, my love and pride for Korean food runs deep and this *Korean Paleo* cookbook is my dream book. Sounds so cheesy but it's true. I first started my Paleo journey in 2012 after self-experimenting and learning about my food sensitivities to gluten and dairy. While I felt better than I had in years, I was heartbroken to realize the considerable amount of soy, wheat and processed ingredients in most Korean food.

Traditional methods of preparing Korean food, like fermenting and soaking, are extremely beneficial for our gut health. However, with modernization comes shortcuts and more processed versions of these time-honored dishes and ingredients. It's hard to find condiments like *gochujang* (red chili paste) and *doenjang* (Korean miso paste) these days that do not contain wheat, corn syrup and other hard-to-digest thickeners and fake sugars. To cut down on costs, these are what most Korean restaurants use; I would feel so bloated and uncomfortable after eating out at these places.

For years, I've been recreating Paleo versions of my favorite Korean dishes at home, but you won't find many of those recipes on my blog that I started in 2014. Why? Well, even way back when my blog was just a baby and the only people that went to look at any of my posts were my then-boyfriend (now husband) and my mom, I had a big, big dream of saving all my Korean Paleo recipes for a cookbook that I'd eventually write.

Well, that day is finally here and I'm so proud to be sharing a piece of my dream with you in this collection of traditional and modern dishes so near and dear to my heart. All the recipes you'll find in this book are 100 percent Paleo, except a few recipes that use mung bean sprouts, which are in the gray area, but they are nutritious and easy to digest. If you run into ingredients that you aren't familiar with, you can refer to the Stocking Up Your Korean Paleo Kitchen section (pages 185 to 187) at the back of the book, which explains how they are used, as well as where you can purchase some of these ingredients. Even with the grain-free substitutions, you'll find that the flavors are still authentic and true to the elements of the original recipes.

While there are staple dishes, each household has its own unique version of preparing them, and mine is heavily influenced by my mom's and grandmother's methods. I hope these recipes introduce you to the beautiful world of Korean cuisine that represents so much care, healing and mother's love.

Happy cooking,

Jean

COOKING WITH BAP
(Rice Dishes)

Rice is a staple of Korean cooking and historically symbolizes wealth and prosperity. It's so much a part of the culture that my grandmother would hand us cooked rice as kids to use as glue for school projects (I'm sure my fellow Koreans are laughing about this relatable memory).

Bap means "cooked rice" while ssal refers to the uncooked version. Bap also means food in general. No matter what you'll be eating, if you are hungry, you say "let's go eat bap" or "do you want to go eat bap?" All the recipes in this chapter are Paleofied by using cauliflower rice; I'm so proud of how delicious and authentic they still taste that I hope you enjoy them as well. There's the classic Bibimbap (page 11), which many of you are probably familiar with, and my personal favorites like Kimchi Bokkeumbap (Kimchi Fried Rice) (page 12), Korean Curry Rice (page 19) and Kongnamul Bap (Bean Sprout Rice Bowl) (page 20).

BIBIMBAP
(Mixed Rice Bowl)

Bibimbap is one of the most popular Korean dishes in the Western world. It's a recipe that's easy to put together, especially if you have some banchan (side dishes) premade and ready to go in the fridge. You can easily adjust the seasoning and spices to your liking.

Serves 1

½ cup (60 g) thinly sliced cucumber

⅛ tsp sea salt, plus more to taste

2 tsp (10 ml) cooking oil, divided

1 small carrot, julienned

1 egg

Ground black pepper, to taste

1 cup (160 g) Cauliflower Sticky Rice (page 182)

½ cup (125 g) Bulgogi (BBQ Beef) (page 28), chopped into 1″ (2.5-cm) pieces

¼ cup (25 g) packed Sukju Namul (Mung Bean Sprout Salad) (page 126)

¼ cup (57 g) packed Sigeumchi Namul (Spinach Salad) (page 106)

¼ cup (28 g) thinly sliced Gim Gui (Roasted Seaweed) (page 129)

½ tsp toasted sesame seeds

2 tsp (10 ml) Gochujang (Korean Red Chili Paste) (page 174), or more to taste

2 tsp (10 ml) toasted sesame oil, or more to taste

Sprinkle the cucumber slices with ⅛ teaspoon of sea salt and let them sit for 15 minutes. Squeeze the water out of the cucumber with your hands and set aside.

Heat 1 teaspoon of cooking oil in a skillet over medium-high heat. Add the carrot to the skillet, sprinkle with sea salt and saute for 2 to 3 minutes until tender but still crunchy. Remove from the heat and set aside.

Heat the remaining 1 teaspoon of cooking oil over medium-low heat in the same skillet and crack an egg in it, being careful not to break the yolk. Season with salt and pepper and fry for 3 to 5 minutes, until the white is set and the yolk is still runny. Remove from the heat and set aside.

Assemble the Bibimbap bowl: Place the Cauliflower Sticky Rice at the bottom of a large bowl. Layer with the Bulgogi, salted cucumber slices, julienned carrot, Sukju Namul, Sigeumchi Namul and Gim Gui. Lay the egg on the top and sprinkle with toasted sesame seeds. Add the Gochujang and toasted sesame oil. Mix everything together and taste. Add more Gochujang and/or toasted sesame oil, if needed, then mix again and serve.

KIMCHI BOKKEUMBAP

(Kimchi Fried Rice)

When most people think of comfort food, it's something along the lines of tomato soup with grilled cheese or some kind of casserole. For me, it's this freshly prepared Kimchi Bokkeumbap. There's something about cooked kimchi, bacon and "rice" that immediately makes me think of home, and I wouldn't have it any other way.

Serves 4

1 medium head cauliflower

4 slices thick-cut bacon, chopped

2 cloves garlic, minced

½ medium onion, chopped

1 cup (150 g) well-fermented and sour kimchi, drained and chopped

3 tbsp (45 ml) kimchi juice

1 tbsp (15 ml) coconut aminos

Salt, to taste

Gochujang (Korean Red Chili Paste) (page 174), optional

1 tsp cooking oil

2 tsp (10 ml) toasted sesame oil

1 tbsp (8 g) toasted sesame seeds

1 green onion, thinly sliced

4 eggs

Salt and pepper, to taste

Thinly sliced Gim Gui (Roasted Seaweed) (page 129), for garnish

Remove the leaves from the cauliflower and cut off the florets from the roots. Using a cheese grater or a food processor with a grater attachment, grate the cauliflower pieces into the size of rice. Set aside.

Heat a large skillet over medium-high heat. Add the chopped bacon and cook, stirring, for 2 to 3 minutes, until browned but still soft. Add the garlic and cook for 30 seconds, then add the onion and chopped kimchi. Saute for 5 minutes.

Add the cauliflower rice, kimchi juice and coconut aminos. Cook, stirring, for 5 minutes or until the cauliflower is cooked through, but not mushy. Taste the rice and add salt if needed. If you would like a spicier Kimchi Bokkeumbap, stir in ½ teaspoon of Gochujang at a time until it reaches your desired spice level. Turn off the heat and stir in the sesame oil, sesame seeds and green onion.

In a separate skillet, heat the cooking oil over medium-low heat. Crack the eggs gently into the pan so you don't break the yolks. Season with salt and pepper, and let the eggs cook for 3 to 5 minutes, until the whites are set but the yolks are still runny.

Divide the Kimchi Bokkeumbap into 4 separate bowls. Top each Kimchi Bokkeumbap bowl with an egg. Garnish with Gim Gui slices.

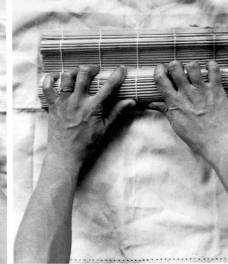

CLASSIC BULGOGI KIMBAP

(Korean Sushi)

Mmmm . . . kimbap. It's a Korean version of sushi that's way more humble. Kimbap is considered a quick and easy finger food on the go or for a picnic, and it's also a popular lunch box meal. This classic style has Bulgogi for the filling, but you can find all different and creative varieties being sold at kimbap specialty shops commonly found in Korea.

Serves 4-5

1 tsp sea salt, divided

1 batch Cauliflower Sticky Rice (page 182), warm

1 kirby cucumber, cut into ¼" (6-mm) strips

2 tsp (10 ml) cooking oil, divided

1 large carrot, julienned

3 eggs

Water, to seal

5 sheets of dry unseasoned seaweed (also called gim or nori)

½ batch Bulgogi (BBQ Beef) (page 28)

5 strips Danmuji (Sweet Pickled Radish) (page 109)

1 batch Sigeumchi Namul (Spinach Salad) (page 106)

Sesame oil

Danmuji (Sweet Pickled Radish) (page 109) rounds, for serving

Add ½ teaspoon of sea salt to the Cauliflower Sticky Rice and stir together. Let it cool.

Place the cucumber strips in a bowl and sprinkle with ¼ teaspoon of sea salt. Let it sit for 10 minutes. Pat dry with paper towels.

Heat 1 teaspoon of cooking oil in a large skillet. Add the carrots with ⅛ teaspoon of sea salt and saute for 3 minutes. Set aside and let it cool.

Whisk together the eggs with ⅛ teaspoon of sea salt until well combined. Heat 1 teaspoon of cooking oil in a 10- to 12-inch (25- to 30-cm) skillet over medium-low heat. Pour the eggs in and let them spread in a thin layer. Cook for 2 minutes until the edges are cooked through, then carefully flip and cook the other side for 2 minutes until cooked through. Remove from the heat, let the eggs cool for 10 minutes, then slice them into ¼-inch (6-mm) strips.

Make the kimbap. For best results, use a sushi rolling mat. Prepare a small bowl of water. Lay down a seaweed sheet on the mat, and spread out ⅔ cup (106 g) of Cauliflower Sticky Rice on the nori sheet, leaving about 2 to 3 inches (5 to 7.5 cm) of space on the top part of the sheet. Add a line of Bulgogi on top of the rice at the bottom edge of the nori sheet. Then add a strip of Danmuji, cucumber strips, julienned carrots, Sigeumchi Namul and strips of eggs. Lift up the bottom edge of the mat, then start rolling as you press down on the fillings with your fingers. Wrap the mat over the first roll, pressing down firmly to make it tight. As you continuously roll and approach the top of the nori sheet, wet the top edge with a bit of water so the seam sticks at the end. Brush the outside lightly with sesame oil. Repeat with the rest of the nori sheets and ingredients.

Once finished, slice each roll into ½-inch (12-mm) slices and serve with Danmuji rounds.

*See photo on page 17 (roll on the right).

SPICY TUNA AND KIMCHI KIMBAP

This kimbap is a simpler and spicier kimbap that's just as delicious. With the addition of kimchi, you really don't need that many ingredients to make this recipe shine.

Serves 4

½ tsp sea salt

1 batch Cauliflower Sticky Rice (page 182), warm

2 (5-oz [142-g]) cans tuna

6 tbsp (90 ml) Gochujang Mayonnaise (page 151)

2 tsp (10 ml) Dijon mustard

Water, to seal

4 sheets of dry unseasoned seaweed (also called gim or nori)

¾ cup (112.5 g) chopped kimchi

Sesame oil

Danmuji (Sweet Pickled Radish) (page 109) rounds, for serving

Add the sea salt to the Cauliflower Sticky Rice and stir. Let cool.

Drain the cans of tuna and mix the tuna with the Gochujang Mayonnaise and Dijon mustard until well combined.

Make the kimbap. For best results, use a sushi rolling mat. Prepare a small bowl of water. Lay down a seaweed sheet on the mat, and spread out ⅔ cup (106 g) of rice on the nori sheet, leaving about 2 to 3 inches (5 to 7.5 cm) of space on the top part of the sheet. Add a line of spicy tuna. Then, add a line of chopped kimchi. Lift up the bottom edge of the mat, then start rolling as you press down on the fillings with your fingers. Wrap the mat over the first roll, pressing down firmly to make it tight. As you continuously roll and approach the top of the seaweed sheet, wet the top edge with a bit of water so the seam sticks at the end. Brush the outside lightly with sesame oil. Repeat with the rest of the seaweed sheets and ingredients.

Once finished, slice each roll into ½-inch (12-mm) slices, and serve with Danmuji rounds.

KOREAN CURRY RICE

Curry rice in Korea is made from a very popular instant curry mix sold prepackaged at grocery stores, and I used to eat it all the time growing up. It comes in a large pouch, which you heat up and pour over rice that you prepare separately. I remember being so sad to find out that it uses gluten as a thickener. Fortunately, this clean, wheat-free version tastes so much like the real thing, and I was so happy creating this dish, that I may have made it three times in one week.

Serves 4

1 tbsp (15 ml) cooking oil

1 lb (454 g) boneless beef short ribs, or chicken breasts or thighs, cubed

1 large onion, diced

2 medium potatoes, peeled and cubed

2 carrots, chopped into ¼" (6-mm) pieces

2 cloves garlic, minced

1 tsp sea salt, or more to taste

3 cups (720 ml) water, divided

¼ cup (32 g) coconut flour

2 tbsp (13 g) oriental curry powder or regular curry powder

1 tbsp (12.5 g) coconut sugar

1 tbsp (7 g) onion powder

1 tbsp (7 g) garlic powder

2 tsp (6 g) turmeric

1 tsp ground black pepper

Cauliflower Sticky Rice (page 182) and kimchi, for serving

Heat the cooking oil in a Dutch oven over medium-high heat. Add the meat and diced onion and cook, stirring, for about 5 minutes, until the meat is browned. Add the potatoes, carrots and garlic, then cook, stirring, for 5 minutes.

Add the sea salt and 2 cups (480 ml) of water, and bring to a boil. Once boiling, lower the heat to medium-low and simmer for 10 minutes.

In the meantime, make the curry sauce by combining 1 cup (240 ml) of water, the coconut flour, curry powder, coconut sugar, onion powder, garlic powder, turmeric and ground black pepper. Whisk together until thickened.

Add the curry sauce to the Dutch oven and stir to combine. Let this simmer for 15 minutes until reduced and slightly thickened. Taste and add more salt, if needed.

Serve over Cauliflower Sticky Rice with a side of kimchi.

KONGNAMUL BAP

(Bean Sprout Rice Bowl)

This rice bowl is usually made with soybean sprouts, but to make it a bit more Paleo-friendly, I decided to use mung bean sprouts. While some may argue that they aren't entirely Paleo, mung bean sprouts are extremely nutritious and delicious, and I couldn't not include one of my favorite Korean recipes. In a way, it's a simplified version of bibimbap, but the flavors are anything but simple.

Serves 4

1 batch Cauliflower Sticky Rice (page 182)

Mixing Sauce
5 tbsp (75 ml) coconut aminos

2 tsp (10 ml) sesame oil

2 tsp (5 g) toasted sesame seeds

½ tsp sea salt

½ tsp honey

½ tsp gochugaru

1 clove garlic, minced

2 green onions, chopped

1 lb (454 g) ground beef

2 tbsp (30 ml) coconut aminos

2 tsp (10 ml) apple cider vinegar or coconut vinegar

1 tsp sesame oil

½ tsp sea salt

¼ tsp ground black pepper

2 cloves garlic, minced

2 tbsp (30 ml) cooking oil, divided

1 lb (454 g) mung bean sprouts

Kimchi, for serving

Prepare the Cauliflower Sticky Rice. Make the mixing sauce by combining the coconut aminos, sesame oil, sesame seeds, sea salt, honey, gochugaru, garlic and green onions in a bowl.

Combine the ground beef with the coconut aminos, vinegar, sesame oil, sea salt, black pepper and garlic, and mix well. Heat 1 tablespoon (15 ml) of cooking oil in a large skillet over medium-high heat. Add the beef mixture and stir-fry until fully browned and cooked through. Remove from the skillet, drain and set aside.

In the same skillet, heat 1 tablespoon (15 ml) of cooking oil. Add the mung bean sprouts and stir-fry for 5 minutes, until they turn translucent and soft. Remove from the heat.

When ready to serve, divide the Cauliflower Sticky Rice into 4 bowls. Layer the beef on top of the rice, then the mung bean sprouts on top of the beef. Drizzle the mixing sauce over everything and serve with a side of kimchi. Mix everything together before digging in!

OMURICE
(Omelet Fried Rice)

Omurice is one of those dishes that every Korean kid goes crazy over when it's put in front of them. Any kind of Western or fusion food is such a treat, especially because the most popular version of omurice is made with Spam (that is . . . if your parents were REAL cool). I used high-quality ham instead in this recipe, and the result took me right back to my simple childhood days when getting fried rice wrapped in eggs would be the highlight of my day.

Serves 2

Paleo Ketchup

1 (6-7 oz [170–198 g]) can or jar of tomato paste

¼ cup (60 ml) water, or more

3 tbsp (45 ml) apple cider vinegar

1 tbsp (15 ml) maple syrup

1 tsp garlic powder

1 tsp onion powder

½ tsp sea salt

½ large head cauliflower

1 tbsp + 2 tsp (25 ml) cooking oil, divided

¾ cup (115 g) ham, cubed

½ onion, diced

2 cloves garlic, minced

1 carrot, diced

½ red bell pepper, chopped

1 tbsp (15 ml) coconut aminos

1 tbsp (15 ml) apple cider vinegar

2 green onions, chopped

4 eggs

¼ tsp sea salt

⅛ tsp ground black pepper

Use your ketchup of choice or make my Paleo version ahead of time: Combine the tomato paste and water in a saucepan and heat over medium heat. Just as the mixture starts to boil, turn off the heat. Add the apple cider vinegar, maple syrup, garlic powder, onion power and sea salt and stir well. Cool to room temperature. Stir in more water if you want a thinner consistency, and store in an airtight container in the refrigerator for 3 to 4 weeks.

Remove the leaves from the cauliflower and cut off the florets from the roots. Use a cheese grater or a food processor with a grater attachment to grate the cauliflower into the size of rice. Set aside.

Heat 1 tablespoon (15 ml) of cooking oil in a skillet over medium-high heat. Add the ham, onion, garlic, carrot and red bell pepper, and stir-fry until the vegetables are soft and translucent, about 5 minutes. Add the cauliflower rice, coconut aminos and apple cider vinegar, and cook, stirring, for about 5 minutes, until the cauliflower is soft and cooked through. Add the green onions, stir a few times and take off the heat.

In a bowl, crack the eggs and add the salt and pepper. Whisk until well combined.

Heat 1 teaspoon of cooking oil in a 10-inch (25-cm) nonstick skillet over medium-low heat. Add half of the egg mixture and tilt the pan to spread out the eggs into a thin circle. After about 2 minutes, the bottom of the eggs should set while the top is still slightly runny. Add half the fried rice over one half of the eggs. Fold the eggs from the other side so you have a semicircular omelet with fried rice in the middle, kind of like a taco. Carefully slide the Omurice onto a serving plate. Repeat with the second half of the eggs and fried rice.

Add ketchup to the top of the omelet before serving. You can eat Omurice on its own, or with a banchan of your choice.

BBQS AND SO MUCH MORE

(Protein Dishes)

When most people think of Korean protein dishes, they immediately think of Korean barbecue. While, yes, Korean barbecue is abso-freakin-lutely delicious and fun to eat, and it's grown so much in popularity for those reasons, there are so many other lesser-known dishes that are worth trying out, like Yangnyeom Tongdak (Sweet and Spicy Crispy Chicken Wings) (page 32), Bossam (Pork Belly Wraps) (page 47) and Mandu (Meat and Kimchi Dumplings) (page 51).

In this chapter, you'll find all different types of meats and fish cooked using various methods like braising, deep-frying, stir-frying and grilling. I even threw in some slow cooker and Instant Pot methods so you can taste the authentic flavors with half the amount of work. I hope it helps you expand your mind and palate to new-to-you dishes. Be sure to share them with your friends and family because trying a new cuisine is the best way to experience that culture and connect with your loved ones!

DWEIJI BULGOGI

(Spicy Pork BBQ)

Happiness is . . . spicy, fatty pork, grilled to perfection. I think that's the saying, right? But in all seriousness, this is one of my favorite barbecue dishes and you know I'm not leaving a Korean BBQ table until I get my fill of Dweiji Bulgogi. Not only is it insanely addicting, it's one of the rare times that I prefer pork over beef when it comes to grilled meats.

Serves 3–4

1 lb (454 g) pork belly, neck or shoulder, thinly sliced (about ¼" [6 mm] thick)

Marinade
3 tbsp (45 ml) Gochujang (Korean Red Chili Paste) (page 174)

2 tbsp (30 ml) coconut aminos

2 tbsp (30 ml) apple cider vinegar or coconut vinegar

1 tbsp (8 g) gochugaru, or more if you like spicy

2 tsp (10 ml) honey

1 tsp sesame oil

¼ tsp ground black pepper

3 cloves garlic, minced

½" (12-mm) piece fresh ginger, minced

1 small onion, sliced

2 green onions, cut into 1–2" (2.5–5-cm) pieces

1 tsp cooking oil, if pan-frying

Toasted sesame seeds, for garnish

Cauliflower Sticky Rice (page 182) and/or red or green leaf lettuce, for serving

Start by cutting the pork into 2- to 3-inch (5- to 7.5-cm) pieces.

For the marinade, combine the Gochujang, coconut aminos, vinegar, gochugaru, honey, sesame oil, black pepper, garlic and ginger in a large bowl and mix well. Add the pork, onion and green onions, and mix until the meat and the vegetables are coated. Cover, and let it marinate in the refrigerator for at least 1 hour.

When ready to cook, heat the grill over medium-high heat. Right before cooking the meat, reduce the heat to medium, then grill the meat for about 7 to 8 minutes, flipping halfway through. If pan-frying, heat cooking oil in a pan over medium-high heat, then lower the heat to medium right before you lay the meat on the pan. Cook the meat in batches so you don't crowd the pan. Cook for about 7 to 8 minutes, flipping halfway through.

Sprinkle with toasted sesame seeds before serving. Serve with Cauliflower Sticky Rice and/or lettuce to eat as lettuce wraps.

BULGOGI
(BBQ Beef)

Probably one of the most popular barbecue meats, Bulgogi is a traditional Korean dish known for its addictive sweet and salty combo. The trick is to slice the meat paper-thin so it can soak up as much of the delicious marinade as possible. You can probably find these meats pre-sliced at a local Korean grocery store, but if not, you can easily do this at home by freezing the meat slightly first.

Serves 3-4

1 lb (454 g) beef sirloin (or any other tender cuts that are well marbled)

Marinade

6 tbsp (90 ml) coconut aminos

½ medium pear (preferably Korean pear), cut into chunks

2 tsp (10 ml) sesame oil

1" (2.5-cm) piece fresh ginger

3 cloves garlic, peeled

2 tbsp (30 ml) apple cider vinegar or coconut vinegar

½ tsp sea salt

¼ tsp ground black pepper

1 medium onion, sliced

2 green onions, sliced in 1" (2.5-cm) pieces

1 carrot, sliced

1 tbsp (15 ml) cooking oil

1 tbsp (8 g) toasted sesame seeds, for serving

Green or red leaf lettuce and Umma's Ssamjang (Dipping Sauce) (page 178), optional

Place the beef in the freezer for 30 minutes, then take it out and slice it thinly, about ⅟₁₆ to ⅛ inch (1 to 3 mm) thick.

Place the coconut aminos, pear, sesame oil, ginger, garlic, vinegar, sea salt and black pepper in a high-powered blender. Blend well until liquified.

Combine the sliced beef and the marinade in a large bowl. Toss and massage together with your hand until all the beef slices are covered in the marinade. Cover and marinate in the refrigerator for 1 hour to overnight.

When you are ready to cook the beef, remove it from the marinade, shaking off the excess. Slice the onion, green onions and carrot, and combine the vegetables with the meat.

Heat the cooking oil over high heat in a large skillet. Working in batches so you don't overcrowd the pan, add the beef and vegetables and stir-fry together until the meat is browned and cooked through, about 5 to 7 minutes.

Sprinkle with toasted sesame seeds before serving. You can eat Bulgogi on its own or in a lettuce wrap served with Umma's Ssamjang (Dipping Sauce).

LA GALBI
(BBQ Short Ribs)

"Galbi" in Korean literally translates to "ribs," and LA galbi is just beef short ribs cut thinly across the bones. Why LA? This unique cut was originated and popularized by Korean immigrants decades back in Los Angeles. You can easily find it at Korean grocery stores, but if not, just explain to the butcher how you want the short ribs to be cut. Also, you are doing it wrong if you use utensils to eat LA Galbi. The bone is there so you can hold it with your fingers while you tear into the meat. It's the only way to eat it!

Serves 4

3 lb (1.3 kg) short ribs, cut across the bones, about ¼–⅓" (6–8-mm) thick

Marinade
⅔ cup (160 ml) coconut aminos

¼ cup (60 ml) water

½ large onion, cut into chunks

2 tbsp (30 ml) apple cider vinegar or coconut vinegar

2 tbsp (30 ml) sesame oil

4 cloves garlic

1" (2.5-cm) piece fresh ginger

1 tbsp (15 ml) maple syrup

1 tsp black pepper

1 tbsp (15 ml) cooking oil, if panfrying

1 green onion, chopped, for garnish

Place the short ribs in a large resealable bag.

For the marinade, add the coconut aminos, water, onion, vinegar, sesame oil, garlic, ginger, maple syrup and black pepper to a blender and blend until smooth. Pour the marinade into the bag with the short ribs and seal. Transfer to the refrigerator and marinate for 1 hour to overnight.

Remove the beef from the refrigerator 30 minutes before cooking. Preheat the grill over medium-high heat. Grill the beef for 2 to 3 minutes on each side, until cooked through and slightly charred. You can also pan-fry them with 1 tablespoon (15 ml) of cooking oil in a skillet over medium-high heat for the same amount of time.

Before serving, cut the meat so each section contains a bone. Garnish with chopped green onion.

YANGNYEOM TONGDAK

(Sweet and Spicy Crispy Chicken Wings)

Chicken wings are considered to be one of those delicious, treat-yo-self junk foods in Korea. In recent years, their popularity exploded in the United States, and it's relatively easy to find Korean wing restaurants in major cities. While they are usually deep-fried to yummy crispiness before getting coated with the magical spicy sauce, you can easily achieve the same result at home by baking them on high heat and whipping up the sauce using some simple ingredients.

Serves 2-3

2 lb (908 g) chicken wings

1 tbsp (12 g) baking powder

½ tsp sea salt

Wing Sauce

3 tbsp (45 ml) Gochujang
(Korean Red Chili Paste) (page 174)

2 tbsp (30 ml) honey

2 tbsp (30 ml) apple cider vinegar or
coconut vinegar

2 tbsp (30 ml) coconut aminos

1 tbsp (15 ml) fish sauce

1 tsp gochugaru

1 tbsp (15 ml) sesame oil

½ tsp ground black pepper

2 cloves garlic, minced

½" (12-mm) piece fresh ginger, minced

Toasted sesame seeds, for garnish

Thinly sliced green onion, for garnish

Preheat the oven to 425°F (218°C). Line a baking sheet with parchment paper or aluminum foil and place an oven-safe wire rack over it.

Pat the wings dry and place them in a large bowl. Sprinkle the wings with baking powder and sea salt and toss until the wings are evenly coated. Place the wings on the wire rack, laying them down so they don't touch each other. Bake the wings for 40 minutes, flipping halfway through.

While the wings are baking, mix together the Gochujang, honey, vinegar, coconut aminos, fish sauce, gochugaru, sesame oil, black pepper, garlic and ginger until they are well combined.

When the wings are finished cooking, transfer them to a large mixing bowl. Pour the sauce over the wings and toss together until the wings are well coated. Sprinkle with sesame seeds and green onions. Serve immediately.

DOENJANG GUI

(Doenjang Marinated Meat)

Doenjang Gui is a great option for anyone who wants a flavorful grilled meat without the spiciness. The doenjang marinade is excellent on both pork and chicken; it provides a delicious umami flavor without overpowering the taste of the meat.

Serves 3-4

Doenjang Marinade

3 tbsp (45 ml) coconut aminos

2 tbsp (34 g) Paleo Doenjang (Korean Miso Paste) (page 177)

2 tbsp (30 ml) apple cider vinegar or coconut vinegar

1 tbsp (15 ml) honey

¼ medium onion

3 green onions, roughly chopped

3 cloves garlic, peeled

1 lb (454 g) pork belly, thinly sliced (about ¼" [6 mm] thick) or 1 lb (454 g) boneless, skinless chicken thighs

1 tsp cooking oil for pork belly or 1 tbsp (15 ml) cooking oil for chicken thighs, if pan-frying

Chopped green onions and sesame seeds, for garnish

Cauliflower Sticky Rice (page 182), Umma's Ssamjang (Dipping Sauce) (page 178) and/or red or green leaf lettuce, for serving

For the doenjang marinade, place the coconut aminos, Paleo Doenjang, vinegar, honey, onion, green onions and garlic in a blender and blend until thick and smooth. If using chicken, use a meat pounder to flatten the meat into an even layer.

Place the meat in a large container or a resealable plastic bag. Pour the blended marinade over the meat and massage to coat. Let this sit in the refrigerator for 1 hour to overnight, turning over the meat halfway through.

When ready to cook, heat the grill over medium-high heat. Right before cooking the meat, reduce the heat to medium. Grill the pork for 7 to 8 minutes, flipping halfway through, or if using chicken, grill for 11 to 12 minutes, flipping halfway through.

If pan-frying, heat the cooking oil in a pan over medium-high heat, then lower the heat to medium right before you lay the meat on the pan. Cook the meat in the pan in batches so you don't crowd the pan. Cook the pork for about 7 to 8 minutes, flipping halfway through, or if using chicken, cook for 11 to 12 minutes, flipping halfway through.

Cut into bite-sized pieces and sprinkle with chopped green onions and sesame seeds before serving. You can eat it with a side of Cauliflower Sticky Rice and dip it in Umma's Ssamjang (Dipping Sauce), or wrap it in a lettuce wrap.

DWEJI GALBI KIMCHI JJIM

(Kimchi Braised Pork Ribs)

This might be one of the simplest main dish recipes. It only takes five ingredients (one being water . . . so does that really count?), but it's actually the biggest crowd pleaser. There's something so tasty and amazing when pork and kimchi come together, especially when they are braised for a long time. My mom would make this when she was too busy or just lazy, and all of us would devour everything to the last drop. This recipe can be easier if you use the Instant Pot, and I've included instructions for it as well.

Serves 2-3

2 lb (908 g) pork ribs

1 large onion, sliced

4 cups (600 g) well-fermented and sour kimchi, including the juice

Water, for stove top method

1 green onion, chopped

Cauliflower Sticky Rice (page 182), for serving

Stovetop Method

Fill a heavy-bottomed pot or a Dutch oven two-thirds full of water. Heat over medium-high heat until it comes to a boil. Add the pork ribs. Reduce the heat to medium-low, cover and let simmer for 30 minutes. Drain the ribs and set aside. Discard the water.

Add the onion slices to the bottom of the same pot. Place the pork ribs on top of the onion slices. Then add the kimchi on top of the pork. Add enough water to cover the onion and the pork, but not the kimchi. Cover and bring to a boil over medium-high heat. Reduce the heat to low and let it simmer for 30 minutes. Check every 10 minutes, and add more water if needed.

Once the pork is tender, remove it from the heat. Transfer it to a large serving bowl and sprinkle with chopped green onion. Serve with Cauliflower Sticky Rice.

Instant Pot Method

Add the onion slices to the bottom of the Instant Pot. Place the pork ribs on top of the onion slices. Then, add the kimchi on top of the pork. You don't need to add any liquid as the pork and kimchi will create its own while cooking. If it doesn't come to pressure, add more kimchi juice, just enough to cover the bottom of the pot.

Close the lid, then make sure the pressure valve is sealed. Cook on high on manual pressure for 30 minutes. Once it beeps, release the pressure manually.

Open the lid, transfer the mixture to a large serving bowl and sprinkle with chopped green onion. Serve with Cauliflower Sticky Rice.

> **Tip:** If the kimchi you use is overly fermented, it might yield a dish that's a bit too sour for your taste. If this happens, you can stir in a little bit of coconut sugar to the final product to offset the sourness.

DAKKOCHI

(Spicy Chicken BBQ Skewers)

I think food on sticks is a concept that is loved universally because it's so much fun—Korea is no exception. Dakkochi is a sold by street food vendors and is commonly eaten as "anju," or snacks to accompany your alcoholic beverage. There are many variations of the sauce, but you can never go wrong with this classic spicy version with a hint of sweetness.

Serves 6-8

Marinade

½ cup (112 g) pineapple chunks, fresh or canned

3 tbsp (45 ml) Gochujang (Korean Red Chili Paste) (page 174)

1 tbsp (15 ml) avocado oil

4 cloves garlic, peeled

1" (2.5-cm) piece fresh ginger

2 tbsp (30 ml) coconut aminos

2 tbsp (30 ml) fish sauce

2 lb (908 g) chicken breasts or thighs, cut into 1–2" (2.5–5-cm) pieces

4 green onions, cut into 1" (2.5-cm) pieces

Toasted sesame seeds, for garnish

In a blender, combine the pineapple chunks, Gochujang, avocado oil, garlic cloves, ginger, coconut aminos and fish sauce. Blend until the mixture becomes thick and creamy.

Place the chicken pieces in a wide shallow bowl or a plastic resealable bag, and pour the marinade over the chicken. Massage everything together until all the chicken pieces are covered with the marinade. Transfer to the refrigerator and let it marinate for 30 minutes to 1 hour.

If you are using bamboo skewers, soak them in water 30 minutes before cooking. Remove the chicken from the refrigerator. Shake off the excess marinade from the chicken and start threading them onto the skewers. Alternate between chicken and 2 green onion pieces.

Preheat the grill to medium-high heat. Grill the chicken for 12 to 15 minutes, turning every 4 to 5 minutes. Remove the chicken from the grill when the pieces are charred and cooked through.

Sprinkle with toasted sesame seeds before serving.

GALBIJJIM

(Braised Beef Short Ribs)

Galbijjim is one of those celebratory foods in Korea made over the holidays and other major get-togethers. The braising of this meat makes it fall-off-the-bone tender, and the sauce created during the process is out-of-this-world delicious. While the traditional method of cooking Galbijjim can take a long time with multiple steps, it couldn't get much easier if you use the slow cooker or the Instant Pot.

Serves 4-5

4 lb (1.7 kg) beef short ribs

2 tsp (12 g) sea salt

½ tsp ground black pepper

Sauce

½ medium pear (preferably Korean pear), cut into chunks

½ cup (120 ml) bone broth or beef broth

½ cup (120 ml) coconut aminos

4 cloves garlic

1″ (2.5-cm) piece fresh ginger

1 tbsp (15 ml) fish sauce

1 tbsp (30 ml) apple cider vinegar or coconut vinegar

1 lb (454 g) Korean or daikon radish, cut into chunks

2 carrots, cut into chunks

1 onion, sliced

2 green onions, chopped

If the short ribs aren't cut up already, slice them into sections, so each section contains a bone. Evenly sprinkle them with sea salt and pepper. Set aside.

Make the sauce by combining the pear, broth, coconut aminos, garlic, ginger, fish sauce and vinegar in a blender and blend until thick and smooth.

Slow Cooker Method

Place the short ribs, radish, carrots and onion in the slow cooker. Evenly pour the sauce over everything, then stir to coat. Cook on low for 9 hours, until the meat is fall-off-the-bone tender.

Sprinkle with green onions before serving.

Instant Pot Method

Place the short ribs, radish, carrots and onion in the Instant Pot. Evenly pour the sauce over everything, then stir to coat.

Close the lid and make sure the pressure valve is sealed. Set the Instant Pot to "Meat/Stew" for 35 minutes. Once done cooking, let it sit for 10 to 15 minutes until the pressure naturally releases and you can open the lid easily.

Sprinkle with green onions before serving.

> **Tip:** If you don't love the high fat content of the dish, you can make Galbijjim a day ahead, then drain the liquid that forms and place it in the refrigerator overnight. The fat will float to the top and harden. The next day, remove the fat and add the liquid back in with the meat and vegetables. Reheat and serve.

STICKY "SOY" HONEY DRUMSTICKS

Soy sauce and honey might be one of the most commonly used sauce combos when it comes to Asian cuisines, and for good reason. There's something pretty fabulous about that sweet and salty flavor that's loved by so many. These chicken drumsticks are marinated and cooked until they are deliciously tender, then coated with a thick and sticky "soy" honey sauce for a delicious meal you'll want over and over again.

Serves 4

2 lbs (908 g) chicken drumsticks

½ cup (120 ml) coconut aminos

2 tbsp (30 ml) apple cider vinegar

1 tbsp (15 ml) honey

2 cloves garlic, minced

1" (2.5-cm) piece fresh ginger, minced

Green onions, chopped, for garnish

Toasted sesame seeds, for garnish

Place the chicken drumsticks in a glass container just big enough to lay them in a single layer. Combine and whisk together the coconut aminos, apple cider vinegar, honey, garlic and ginger. Pour over the drumsticks, making sure they are all evenly coated. Place in the refrigerator and marinate for 1 to 4 hours, flipping the chicken halfway through.

Preheat the oven to 400°F (204°C). Line a baking sheet with parchment paper and place the drumsticks on the baking sheet, making sure they aren't touching. Reserve the marinade. Bake the chicken for 40 minutes, flipping the pieces halfway through.

While the chicken is cooking, pour the marinade in a small saucepan and heat on the stovetop over high heat. Once the sauce starts boiling, reduce the heat to medium-low and simmer until the sauce is reduced and thickened, about 7 to 10 minutes.

When the chicken is finished cooking, toss with the reduced sauce. Sprinkle with chopped green onions and toasted sesame seeds before serving.

GODEUNGEO JORIM

(Braised Mackerel and Radish)

Godeungeo Jorim can be served in small amounts as banchan or on a large platter as the main dish. While the mackerel is the star of the dish, I personally love this recipe for the radish that gets so tender and full of flavor during the cooking process. It's one of the most common ways to cook mackerel in Korea, and it was one of my favorite dishes growing up.

Serves 4

2 whole mackerel

1 small Korean or 1 medium daikon radish

Spicy Sauce
4 cloves garlic, minced

1" (2.5-cm) piece fresh ginger, minced

¼ cup (60 ml) coconut aminos

2 tbsp (30 ml) apple cider vinegar or coconut vinegar

1 tbsp (15 ml) Gochujang (Korean Red Chili Paste) (page 174)

1 tbsp (8 g) gochugaru

2 tsp (10 ml) honey

2 cups (480 ml) water

1 onion, sliced

2 red or green chili or jalapeño peppers, optional

2 green onions, chopped into 1–2" (2.5–5-cm) pieces

Cauliflower Sticky Rice (page 182), for serving

If not already cleaned, slice the heads and the fins off the mackerel. Make a slit on the side of the fish and remove the guts. Clean the fish under cold running water, then pat dry with a paper towel. Cut them into 3-inch (7.5-cm) pieces.

Cut the radish crosswise into ½-inch (12-mm) thick rounds. Cut them in half again, so you have half-circle pieces. For the spicy sauce, combine the garlic, ginger, coconut aminos, vinegar, Gochujang, gochugaru and honey in a small bowl and set aside.

Place the radish and 2 cups (480 ml) of water in a saucepan and heat over medium heat. Once it comes to a boil, cover and let it cook for 5 minutes.

Add the mackerel fillets, onion and chili peppers (if using) on top of the radish, then pour the spicy sauce on top. Let the mixture boil for 15 minutes uncovered, without stirring. Occasionally spoon the broth over the mackerel and onions. The sauce should reduce and thicken. Reduce the heat to medium-low, partially cover with a lid and let it simmer for 10 additional minutes.

Add the green onions and let it simmer for 1 more minute. Serve with a side of Cauliflower Sticky Rice.

BOSSAM
(Pork Belly Wraps)

This dish always make me think of my older brother, YoungJae, because I've never met anyone who loves pork belly more. There would always be double servings available just for him, and he would clean the plate in one sitting. Bossam consists of boiled pork belly slices that you wrap in napa cabbage leaves, topped with spicy condiments to balance out the richness of the pork. It's perfection in one bite.

Serves 6–9

½ napa cabbage

¼ cup (60 g) sea salt

2–3 lb (908–1362 g) pork belly

1 onion, quartered

2" (5-cm) piece fresh ginger, sliced

6 cloves garlic, smashed and peeled

2 tbsp (34 g) Paleo Doenjang (Korean Miso Paste) (page 177)

2 tbsp (30 ml) apple cider vinegar or coconut vinegar

1 tbsp (15 ml) coconut aminos

1 tbsp (15 ml) fish sauce

1 tbsp (9 g) whole black peppercorns

1 tbsp (15 ml) honey

6 cups (1.5 L) water, plus more to cover pork

Musaengchae (Sweet and Sour Radish Salad) (page 125), for serving

Kimchi, for serving

Saewoojeot, for serving

Cut the bottom end off the napa cabbage and discard. Remove and discard the outer green leaves, and wash the yellow leaves thoroughly. Place them in a large bowl, and evenly sprinkle them with sea salt and massage to coat. Let this sit for 2 hours, until the leaves are soft and easily bendable. Wash the leaves thoroughly. Place in the refrigerator until ready to use.

For the boiled pork, place the pork belly, onion, ginger, garlic, Paleo Doenjang, vinegar, coconut aminos, fish sauce, peppercorns, honey and 6 cups (1.5 L) of water in a large pot, adding more water if needed to cover the pork. Bring the mixture to a boil over high heat. Lower the heat to medium-low, cover and let the mixture simmer for 1 hour. Turn off the heat and let the pork cool in the broth for 30 minutes before transferring it to a cutting board. Discard the broth and cut the pork belly into ⅛- to ¼-inch (3- to 6-mm) slices.

To eat, place a pork belly slice on top of a cabbage leaf. Add kimchi or Musaengchae on top of the pork, then add a little bit of saewoojeot. Eat it in one bite!

> **Note:** If you can't find saewoojeot, you can omit it or substitute it with a small bowl of sea salt instead.

TANGSUYUK
(Sweet and Sour Fried Pork)

Tangsuyuk is a Chinese-Korean dish that my family would order every time we went to a Chinese restaurant run by Koreans. While it's technically a main dish, it is commonly ordered as an appetizer and served family style. The beauty of this recipe is that the pork is twice fried, making it ultra crispy, then coated with a super thick and yummy sweet and sour sauce. I always had a hard time not overeating these before the main dishes would come out!

Serves 3-4

1 lb (454 g) pork loin, cut into thin strips

½ tsp sea salt

¼ tsp ground black pepper

1 cup (152 g) potato starch (not potato flour)

1 cup (240 ml) filtered water

1 egg

3 cups (720 ml) palm shortening, avocado oil or animal fat, for frying

Tangsuyuk Sauce
1 cup (240 ml) water

1 tbsp + 1 tsp (13 g) potato starch

¼ cup (60 ml) apple cider vinegar or coconut vinegar

2 tbsp (30 ml) coconut aminos

2 tbsp (30 ml) honey

1 tsp sea salt

1 tbsp (15 ml) cooking oil

½ small onion, diced

2 cloves garlic, minced

½ zucchini, thinly sliced

½ carrot, thinly sliced

¼ green bell pepper, diced into ½" (12-mm) squares

¼ red bell pepper, diced into ½" (12-mm) squares

Sprinkle the pork strips evenly with salt and pepper and mix well. Cover and transfer to the refrigerator.

Whisk together the potato starch and water in a bowl, and let this sit at room temperature for 1 hour. The starch will separate from the water and sink to the bottom. Carefully pour out the water. Crack an egg into the soaked starch and use a fork to whisk together until well combined. The starch may seem hardened at first, but it will loosen up as you whisk with a bit of force.

Heat 3 cups (720 ml) of the oil of your choice in a saucepan over medium-high heat until it reaches about 350°F (177°C). Line a large plate with a few layers of paper towels. Remove the pork strips from the refrigerator, add them to the potato starch batter and stir.

Making sure you don't crowd the saucepan, add about 4 of the pork strips into the oil and let them fry until they float to the top and are light yellow in color, about 30 seconds to 1 minute. Remove them from the oil and place on the prepared paper towel-lined plate. Repeat with the rest of the pork.

Let the pork cool for 10 minutes, then deep fry them again, this time in bigger batches. Add about ¼ of the fried pork back into the oil and let it cook through for 3 minutes until golden brown and super crispy. Repeat with the rest of the pork and set aside.

For the Tangsuyuk Sauce, combine the water, potato starch, vinegar, coconut aminos, honey and sea salt in a large bowl. Heat the cooking oil in a deep skillet over medium-high heat. Add the onion, garlic, zucchini, carrot, green and red bell peppers and stir-fry for 3 minutes. Stir the Tangsuyuk Sauce (until it turns cloudy) right before pouring it over the vegetables in the skillet. Let it come to a boil, then reduce the heat to medium-low and let everything simmer for 2 to 3 minutes, until the sauce is thickened. Remove from the heat.

Place the fried pork on a serving plate. Pour the sauce and vegetables over the pork. Serve immediately.

MANDU

(Meat and Kimchi Dumplings)

I still remember for every Lunar New Year, our family would sit together to make dumplings to prepare for another year of luck and prosperity. My mom would then freeze most of the dumplings so we could have a quick meal or a snack when in a pinch for months to come. Because of the nature of the wrapper, you can't steam these, but they are delicious panfried or used in Mandu Guk (Dumpling Soup) (page 60).

Makes approx. 70 dumplings

Filling

1 lb (454 g) ground pork

½ lb (227 g) ground beef

1 cup (150 g) packed sour and well-fermented kimchi, drained and finely chopped

4 oz (112 g) mushrooms, finely chopped

½ small onion, finely chopped

2 green onions, finely chopped

1" (2.5-cm) piece fresh ginger, minced

4 cloves garlic, minced

1 large egg

2 tsp (10 ml) sesame oil

1 tsp sea salt

½ tsp ground black pepper

Dumpling Wrappers

3 cups (366 g) cassava flour

2 tbsp (15 g) tapioca starch

1 tsp sea salt

2 cups (480 ml) hot water

Water, to seal the wrappers

2 tbsp (30 ml) cooking oil

2 tbsp (30 ml) water

Sweet and Sour Dipping Sauce (page 184), for serving

For the filling, combine the ground pork, ground beef, kimchi, mushrooms, onion, green onions, ginger, garlic, egg, sesame oil, sea salt and black pepper in a large bowl and gently mix until well combined. Set aside in the refrigerator until ready to use.

In a large bowl, combine the cassava flour, tapioca starch and sea salt. Add the hot water and mix well until a dough forms. Knead the dough a few times. It may seem slightly dry, but that's okay. Wrap the dough in plastic wrap and let it sit at room temperature for 30 minutes.

Keep the dough in the plastic wrap as you work and prepare a small cup with water. Take a bit of the dough and roll it into a ball about 1 inch (2.5 cm) in diameter. Place the ball between 2 pieces of parchment paper. Use a rolling pin to roll out the dough into a thin circle to make a wrapper, about 3½ to 4 inches (8 to 10 cm) in diameter. Remove the wrapper from the parchment paper and place it gently on your hand.

Add 2 to 3 teaspoons (10 to 15 g) of the filling to the center of the wrapper, then dip your finger in the prepared cup of water. Brush the top half edge of the wrapper with the water where you'll be sealing it. Fold the wrapper in half and pinch the edges to seal completely. Repeat with the rest of the wrappers and filling, placing the dumplings in a single layer and covering them under plastic cling wrap as you work so they don't dry out. Use the dumplings to make Mandu Guk (Dumpling Soup), or follow the next steps to panfry or freeze them.

Heat the cooking oil in a large skillet over medium heat. You'll find that there are 3 sides to dumplings, since they are triangular if you are looking at them from the side. Add the dumplings to the pan in a single layer so they are not touching each other. Cook for 2 minutes, then turn to the second side to cook for 2 additional minutes. Now turn them on their third side to cook for the last 2 minutes.

Add 2 tablespoons (30 ml) of water to the pan, then cover it with a lid. Let it cook for about 1 to 2 minutes until all the water evaporates. Remove from the pan and serve with Sweet and Sour Dipping Sauce.

Freeze for up to 3 months. Thaw on the countertop for 40 minutes before pan-frying, or for 1 hour to use them in Mandu Guk (Dumpling Soup).

KKANPUNG SAEWOO

(Sweet and Spicy Shrimp)

Just like Tangsuyuk (Sweet and Sour Fried Pork) (page 48), Kkanpung Saewoo is originally a Chinese dish that's been altered to better please the Korean palate. Crispy fried shrimp is coated in a sweet and spicy sauce, and it's a unique way to meld together the most delicious flavors and textures.

Serves 4

1 lb (454 g) shrimp, peeled and deveined

Salt and pepper, to taste

1 egg

¼ cup + 2 tbsp (45 g) tapioca starch

2 tbsp (14 g) coconut flour

2 tbsp (30 ml) water

4–5 ice cubes

Avocado oil or palm shortening, for frying

Sauce

3 tbsp (45 ml) coconut aminos

2 tbsp (30 ml) apple cider vinegar or coconut vinegar

2 tbsp (30 ml) hot sauce

1 tbsp (15 ml) water

1 tbsp (15 ml) honey

1 tbsp (15 ml) fish sauce

2 tsp (10 ml) toasted sesame oil

⅛ tsp ground black pepper

1 tsp cooking oil

2 cloves garlic, minced

½ medium onion, chopped

2 cheongyang peppers (or jalapeño or serrano peppers)

½ red bell pepper, chopped

2 green onions, chopped

Toasted sesame seeds, for garnish

Use a paper towel to blot the shrimp dry. Sprinkle lightly with salt and pepper.

In large bowl, combine the egg, tapioca starch, coconut flour and water. Whisk to combine. Add the ice cubes to the batter for extra crispy shrimp.

Pour avocado oil or palm shortening in a large skillet until the oil is about 1 inch (2.5 cm) deep, and heat over medium-high heat. Once the oil is hot, work in batches to not crowd the pan. Coat the shrimp in the batter, then fry in the oil for 30 seconds on each side. Transfer the fried shrimp to a plate in a single layer. Repeat with the rest of the shrimp.

For the sauce, combine the coconut aminos, vinegar, hot sauce, water, honey, fish sauce, sesame oil and black pepper in a bowl. Stir together until the honey is completely dissolved, then set aside.

Heat the cooking oil in a large skillet over medium-high heat. Add the garlic, onion, cheongyang peppers, red bell pepper and green onions, and cook, stirring, for 2 minutes. Pour in the sauce and let it boil until it thickens slightly, about 3 minutes. Add the fried shrimp, then cook, stirring constantly, until the sauce is fully coating the shrimp.

Remove from the heat and sprinkle with toasted sesame seeds before serving.

NAKJI BOKKEUM

(Spicy Stir-Fried Octopus)

If you are a spicy food lover, Nakji Bokkeum may be your jam. Cooking octopus may not be the most comfortable process for many of us, but it's actually a lot easier than you think, and the end result is 100 percent worth it. If you can't handle the spiciness, you can reduce the amount of Gochujang and gochugaru and omit the chili peppers.

Serves 4

1 lb (454 g) baby octopus

Spicy Sauce
2 tbsp (30 ml) Gochujang (Korean Red Chili Paste) (page 174)

2 tsp (5 g) gochugaru

1 tbsp (15 ml) coconut aminos

2 tsp (10 ml) fish sauce

1 tbsp (15 ml) sesame oil

1 tbsp (15 ml) honey

1 tbsp (15 ml) cooking oil

1 onion, sliced

3 cloves garlic, minced

1 carrot, thinly sliced

2 red or green chili or jalapeño peppers, sliced

2 green onions, cut diagonally into 1" (2.5-cm) pieces

Toasted sesame seeds, for garnish

Cauliflower Sticky Rice (page 182), for serving

Rinse the octopus thoroughly under cold running water, then cut into 2- to 3-inch (5- to 7.5-cm) pieces.

For the spicy sauce, combine the Gochujang, gochugaru, coconut aminos, fish sauce, sesame oil and honey and mix well. Mix the octopus pieces with the spicy sauce and let it marinate for 10 minutes.

Heat the cooking oil in a large skillet over medium-high heat. Add the onion, garlic and carrot, and stir-fry for 5 minutes, until the vegetables are tender. Add the chili peppers and cook for 2 minutes. Add the octopus and the sauce. Cook, stirring, for 3 minutes, until the octopus is cooked through. Be careful not to overcook the octopus, as it will get chewy.

Stir in the green onions, then take the skillet off the heat. Sprinkle with toasted sesame seeds and serve with Cauliflower Sticky Rice.

PIPING HOT SOUPS AND STEWS

When it comes to Korean cuisine, you cannot miss out on soups and stews, as they are present at almost every meal. While soups, or guk, are usually individually served so each person has a bowl, stews, or jjigae, are served as a main dish in a big pot so everyone can share at the table. Here, you'll find a bit of both, as well as ones that are served as a meal on their own, like Samgyetang (Ginseng Chicken Soup) (page 64) and Mandu Guk (Dumpling Soup) (page 60).

Koreans are known for their ability to eat extremely high temperature foods, and it still makes me laugh when I take my Midwestern husband to get Korean food and most people are done eating by the time he starts because he's been waiting for his meal to cool down. These scorching soups and stews are even eaten during the summers. There's a phrase, "yi-yeol chi-yeol," which means "fight fire with fire," because it's believed that you can cool down when you eat a hot meal by sweating out the heat in your body. It's actually quite common to hear people say, "Ahhh, it's so cool!" after taking a sip of something steaming hot, which can be confusing for those who don't know this custom.

DOENJANG JJIGAE

(Miso Paste Stew)

You'll find Doenjang Jjigae in every Korean household, and each version is slightly different from the other, depending on the family's secret ingredient or method. Overall, it tastes a bit like Japanese miso soup but stronger and more aromatic, and it's also a bit more complex in flavor from all the vegetables and meat that are added. I think of it as the quintessential Korean comfort food, and for a simple, nourishing meal at home, all you need is a bowl of rice with Doenjang Jjigae and kimchi.

Serves 2

2½ cups (600 ml) water

½ tsp tapioca starch

⅓ cup (10 g) dried anchovies

2 tsp (10 ml) cooking oil

4 oz (114 g) beef stew meat, thinly sliced into bite-sized pieces

1 medium potato, peeled and cut into ½" (12-mm) cubes

½ medium onion, sliced

2 cloves garlic, minced

1 gray zucchini or regular zucchini, quartered lengthwise then sliced

2 tbsp (30 ml) coconut aminos

1 tsp gochugaru

¼ cup (69 g) Paleo Doenjang (Korean Miso Paste) (page 177)

½ batch Hemp Tofu (page 181), sliced into ½" (12-mm) cubes

1 cheongyang or serrano pepper, sliced diagonally

1 green onion, sliced diagonally into 1" (2.5-cm) pieces

Cauliflower Sticky Rice (page 182), for serving

Combine the water, tapioca starch and dried anchovies in a pot and heat over medium-high heat. Once it starts boiling, lower the heat and simmer for 10 minutes. Remove from the heat and discard the anchovies. Set aside the anchovy stock.

In a medium saucepan, heat the cooking oil over medium-high heat. Add the beef, potato, onion and garlic. Cook, stirring, until the meat is browned, about 5 minutes. Add the anchovy stock, zucchini, coconut aminos and gochugaru. Once the mixture starts to boil, reduce the heat to medium, stir in the Paleo Doenjang and let it simmer for 5 minutes.

Add the Hemp Tofu, cheongyang or serrano pepper and green onion, and let it boil for 2 minutes.

Serve with Cauliflower Sticky Rice.

MANDU GUK
(Dumpling Soup)

On the day of Lunar New Year, it's tradition to sit around with your family members and make a giant batch of dumplings, or mandu, together. You freeze most of the dumplings, but reserve some to make this Mandu Guk for that same day. It's so delicious and comforting: like a hug in a bowl.

Serves 2

1 tsp cooking oil

1 egg, whisked

Anchovy Broth

5 cups (1.3 L) water

½ cup (15 g) dried anchovies

6" (15-cm) piece kelp (also called dashima or kombu), optional

½ onion, quartered

3 cloves garlic, smashed and peeled

10 Mandu (Meat and Kimchi Dumplings) (page 51)

2 tbsp (30 ml) coconut aminos

1 tsp sesame oil

½ tsp sea salt

2 green onions, thinly sliced

Gim Gui (Roasted Seaweed) (page 129), thinly sliced, for garnish

Ground black pepper, for garnish

Sweet and Sour Dipping Sauce (page 184), for serving

Kimchi, for serving

Heat the cooking oil over medium-low heat in a large skillet. Once heated, pour in the whisked egg and tilt the pan to spread it out in a thin layer. Cook for 2 minutes, until the egg firms up a bit, then carefully flip it to cook for 2 more minutes. Transfer to a cutting board and slice into thin strips about 2 inches (5 cm) long. Set aside.

For the anchovy broth, combine the water, anchovies, kelp, onion and garlic in a large pot. Bring to a boil over high heat, then reduce the heat to medium-low and simmer for 5 minutes. Remove the kelp from the broth, then let it simmer for 15 more minutes.

Separate the broth from the solids by pouring it through a fine mesh strainer. Discard the solids and return the broth to the pot. Increase the heat to medium-high and wait until the broth comes to a boil.

Add the Mandu (Meat and Kimchi Dumplings) to the broth and give a quick stir so they don't stick to the bottom of the pot. Let them simmer, uncovered, for 4 minutes. Turn off the heat and add in the coconut aminos, sesame oil, sea salt and green onions, and stir together.

Divide the soup between 2 bowls and garnish with the egg slices, Gim Gui slices and ground black pepper. Eat with Sweet and Sour Dipping Sauce, kimchi and/or your favorite banchan as your sides.

KIMCHI JJIGAE
(Kimchi Stew)

Kimchi Jjigae is a super flavorful and deliciously spicy stew that's actually much easier to make than it looks. It's a go-to recipe for when you have old kimchi left that's been well-fermented, and it's a dish beloved by all Koreans, who make it multiple times a week because it's hard to get sick of.

Serves 4

1 tsp cooking oil

½ lb (227 g) pork belly, cut into 1" (2.5-cm) slices

½ onion, sliced thinly

2 cloves garlic, minced

2 cups (300 g) sour fermented kimchi, drained and cut into bite-sized pieces

2 tsp (10 ml) Gochujang (Korean Red Chili Paste) (page 174)

1 tsp gochugaru

½ tsp sea salt

¼ cup (60 ml) kimchi juice

2 cups (480 ml) water, bone broth or chicken broth

¼ batch Hemp Tofu (page 181), cut into ¼–½" (6–12-mm) rectangles

2 green onions, cut into 1" (2.5-cm) slices

Cauliflower Sticky Rice (page 182), for serving

Heat the cooking oil in a pot over medium-high heat. Add the pork belly, onion and garlic, and stir-fry for 4 to 5 minutes, until the pork is browned and the onion slices are softened. Add the kimchi and cook, stirring, for 3 minutes.

Add the Gochujang, gochugaru, sea salt, kimchi juice and water or broth. Stir and let everything come to a boil. Turn down the heat to medium, cover and let it simmer for 15 minutes.

Lay the Hemp Tofu slices on top of the stew. Cover again and let it simmer for 3 minutes.

Add the green onions and take off the heat. Serve hot with a side of Cauliflower Sticky Rice.

SAMGYE-TANG

(Ginseng Chicken Soup)

It's believed that the humid summers of Korea will deplete nutrients from the body through sweating and make you feel run down. To combat this, you eat this nutritious hot soup to replenish the body, regain energy and build stamina. You can taste the subtle earthy and medicinal flavor from the ginseng, but if you can't find fresh ginseng, you can use dried ginseng or omit it altogether for a comforting and tasty chicken soup.

Serves 2

2 cornish hens or 1 (2–3 lb [908–1362 g]) chicken

1 medium head cauliflower

6 cloves garlic, whole

4 dried jujubes (also called red dates)

2 fresh chestnuts, peeled, optional

2 small fresh ginseng roots

8 cups (2 L) water

2 green onions, chopped

Salt and ground black pepper, to taste

Kimchi (page 173 or store-bought), for serving

Remove any giblets from the chicken and wash thoroughly under running water.

Using a cheese grater or a food processor with a grater attachment, grate the cauliflower into the size of rice.

Stuff the poultry cavity with ½ cup (80 g) of grated cauliflower, the garlic cloves, dried jujubes, chestnuts (if using) and ginseng roots. If using 2 cornish hens, divide these ingredients between the 2 birds. Tie the legs together with cotton cooking twine.

Stovetop Method

To cook on the stovetop, transfer the chicken to a large pot. Add the water, cover and heat over medium-high heat until it comes to a boil. Reduce the heat to medium-low and let it simmer for 45 to 50 minutes, until the meat is cooked through and tender. During the last 5 minutes, add the rest of the cauliflower rice into the pot.

Transfer the chicken to a serving bowl, along with the broth. Garnish with the chopped green onions, and serve with small dishes of salt, ground black pepper and kimchi so you can flavor the Samgyetang to your liking.

Instant Pot Method

For the Instant Pot, place the cornish hens or chicken in the Instant Pot, and place the rest of the cauliflower rice around the meat. Add the water, then close the lid, making sure the pressure valve is sealed. Set the Instant Pot to manual pressure on high for 15 minutes. Once it's done cooking, let it sit for 10 minutes until the pressure naturally releases and you can open the lid easily.

Transfer the chicken to a serving bowl, along with the broth. Garnish with the chopped green onions, and serve with small dishes of salt, ground black pepper and kimchi so you can flavor the Samgyetang to your liking. Serve with an empty bowl to discard the bones as you eat.

TIP: If you can only find dried ginseng, soak it overnight before placing it inside the chicken and discard once cooked.

MIYEOK GUK
(Seaweed Soup)

Growing up, it was guaranteed that there would be a hot bowl of Miyeok Guk waiting for us at the breakfast table on our birthdays. Because of the mineral- and nutrient-rich seaweed that's the star of this dish, Miyeok Guk symbolizes birth, and it's even given to new mothers after having a baby for a speedy recovery, as well as on birthdays. The flavor is mild but still quite complex from the simmering of the beef, fish sauce and seaweed. It's a comforting soup that's served frequently and triggers a happy, nostalgic memory for many Koreans.

Serves 4

1.5 oz (43 g) dried seaweed (also called mareun miyeok or wakame)

1 tbsp (15 ml) cooking oil

6 oz (170 g) beef brisket, cut into bite-sized pieces

1 clove garlic, minced

2 tbsp (30 ml) fish sauce

2 tbsp (30 ml) coconut aminos

8 cups (2 L) water

Cauliflower Sticky Rice (page 182), for serving

Kimchi, for serving

Submerge the dried seaweed in water and soak for 30 minutes. The seaweed should hydrate and get much softer and bigger. Drain and rinse under cold water. Cut the seaweed into bite-sized pieces.

Heat the cooking oil in a large pot over medium-high heat. Add the beef and garlic and saute for 5 minutes, until the meat is browned. Add the seaweed, fish sauce, coconut aminos and water. Let the soup come to a boil, then reduce the heat to medium. Cover and let it boil for 25 to 30 minutes, until the beef is tender.

Add more fish sauce and/or coconut aminos, if you want the soup to be saltier. Serve hot with Cauliflower Sticky Rice and kimchi.

DAKDORITANG
(Spicy Chicken Stew)

When my white, Midwestern husband first visited Korea with me, Dakdoritang was the first dish I cooked for him. He kept talking about how spicy it is, but he couldn't stop eating it because it was so freakin' addictive. And that's the best way to describe this stew. Chicken and vegetables are cooked in a flavorful spicy sauce until wonderfully tender, but you'll want a lot of Cauliflower Sticky Rice (page 182) on the side to balance out the heat.

Serves 4-6

3-4 lbs (1.3-1.7 kg) of skin-on cuts of chicken (I use a combination of wings and thighs)

1 tsp sea salt

Spicy Sauce

1 cup (240 ml) chicken broth, bone broth or water

¼ cup (60 ml) coconut aminos

2 tbsp (30 ml) apple cider vinegar

2 tbsp (30 ml) Gochujang (Korean Red Chili Paste) (page 174)

2 tbsp (30 ml) honey

1 tbsp (8 g) gochugaru (omit if you want the stew less spicy)

⅛ tsp ground black pepper

1" (2.5-cm) piece fresh ginger

5 cloves garlic

1 lb (454 g) potatoes, cut into chunks

2 large carrots, cut into 1" (2.5-cm) pieces

2 tbsp (30 ml) cooking oil

1 large onion, cut into chunks

2 green onions, sliced

Toasted sesame seeds, for garnish

If you are using boneless cuts of chicken, cut them into 2-inch (5-cm) pieces, then sprinkle the chicken with sea salt. For the spicy sauce, place the broth (or water), coconut aminos, vinegar, Gochujang, honey, gochugaru, black pepper, ginger and garlic in a blender and blend until smooth.

Slow Cooker Method

Line the bottom of the slow cooker with the potatoes and carrots. Pour half of the spicy sauce over them and mix well.

Heat the cooking oil in a large skillet over medium-high heat. Working in batches, brown the chicken on all sides, about 30 seconds on each side, then remove from the heat.

In a large bowl, combine the chicken, the onion and the rest of the spicy sauce, and mix well. Lay this mixture on top of the potatoes and carrots in the slow cooker, pouring in all the sauce with it.

Cover the slow cooker and cook for 4 hours on high or 6 hours on low. Once finished, garnish with the green onions and toasted sesame seeds before serving.

Instant Pot Method

Set the Instant Pot to the "Sauté" setting, then add the cooking oil and wait about 5 minutes for the liner to heat up and indicate that it's hot. Working in batches, add the chicken and brown on all sides for about 30 seconds on each side. Turn off the Instant Pot and return all the chicken into the liner.

Stir in the potatoes, carrots and onion with the chicken, then pour the spicy sauce over everything. Close the lid, then make sure the pressure valve is sealed. Cook on high on manual pressure for 10 minutes.

Once it beeps to indicate cooking is finished, wait 10 to 15 minutes until the pressure releases naturally and the lid slides open easily. Garnish with the green onions and toasted sesame seeds before serving.

Optional: If you want a thicker stew, you can drain the liquid once the stew is done cooking and simmer it in a saucepan over medium-low heat until thickened to your liking.

HOBAKJUK
(Pumpkin Porridge)

This cozy and comforting fall porridge can be eaten hot or cold, and I remember loving it so much that I would have three full bowls in one sitting as a child. It traditionally uses sweet rice flour to yield a thick and velvety texture, but I found that you can achieve the same result with potato starch. Feel free to leave out the coconut sugar altogether if you like things less sweet. It'll still be naturally sweet and delicious!

Serves 8

2-3 lb (908–1362 g) kabocha or butternut squash, peeled and cubed

3 cups (720 ml) water

2 tbsp (25 g) coconut sugar, plus more to taste

½ tsp sea salt

¼ cup (38 g) potato starch

¼ cup (60 ml) hot water

Pine nuts, toasted sesame seeds, dried jujube slices and/or pumpkin seeds, for garnish

Place the squash cubes in a large pot with the water, cover and bring to a boil over high heat. Reduce the heat to low and simmer for 15 minutes until the squash is tender. Add the coconut sugar and sea salt and use an immersion blender to blend everything until creamy. If you don't have an immersion blender, you can transfer the contents into a regular blender to blend completely, then bring back to the pot to heat.

Increase the heat to medium-high and bring the porridge back to a boil. In a separate bowl, whisk together the potato starch and ¼ cup (60 ml) of hot water until a slurry is formed. Add this to the porridge and stir.

Take off the heat and serve, topped with your favorite garnish. Hobakjuk can be served hot or cold.

YUKGAEJANG

(Korean Spicy Beef Soup)

Yukgaejang is eaten all year round in Korea, and it's a nutritious and delicious spicy dish packed with vegetables. Although fernbrake is a key component of this soup, if you cannot find it easily, you can substitute additional mung bean sprouts. It does take a few hours to make, so make a giant batch for several servings because you'll want more after you try this out!

Serves 4

2 oz (57 g) dried fernbrake or 2 cups (454 g) fresh (also called bracken fiddleheads or gosari)

Beef Broth

1 lb (454 g) beef brisket

1 large onion, quartered

2 cups (232 g) Korean or daikon radish, cut into chunks

5 whole cloves garlic, smashed and peeled

1 tbsp (9 g) black peppercorns

12 cups (3 L) water

8 oz (227 g) mung bean sprouts

12 green onions, cut into 2–3" (5–7.5-cm) pieces

Spicy Sauce

3 tbsp (24 g) gochugaru

2 tbsp (30 ml) coconut aminos

2 tbsp (30 ml) sesame oil

2 tsp (12 g) sea salt

½ tsp ground black pepper

4 cloves garlic, minced

2 eggs

Cauliflower Sticky Rice (page 182), for serving

If you are using dried fernbrake, prepare ahead by soaking them overnight to rehydrate them. They should expand in size. Once rehydrated, cut them into 2- to 3-inch (5- to 7.5-cm) pieces. If you have fresh fernbrake, skip the soaking step and just cut them into 2- to 3-inch (5- to 7.5-cm) pieces.

For the beef broth, place the brisket, onion, radish, garlic, peppercorns and water in a large pot and heat over high heat on the stovetop. Once it starts boiling, decrease the heat to medium-low and let it simmer for 1½ hours. Remove the beef and shred it with 2 forks. If the beef doesn't shred easily, let it simmer longer until it's tender enough. Strain out and discard the vegetables from the broth.

Place the beef in a bowl and add the fernbrake, bean sprouts and green onions. For the spicy sauce, combine the gochugaru, coconut aminos, sesame oil, sea salt, black pepper and garlic. Add the sauce to the bowl with the beef. Mix well with gloved hands until the beef and the vegetables are coated with the sauce.

Add the beef and vegetable mixture back into the pot with the broth. Increase the heat to high, cover and let it come to a boil. Reduce the heat to medium-low and let it simmer for 30 minutes. Taste the soup and adjust seasoning by adding more gochugaru or sea salt, if needed.

In a separate bowl, whisk the eggs together. Slowly drizzle the eggs into the soup and stir a few times so they can cook in the soup.

Take off heat and serve with Cauliflower Sticky Rice.

Tip: If you can't find fernbrake, substitute with 4 ounces (114 g) of additional mung bean sprouts.

KONGNAMUL GUK

(Bean Sprout Soup)

Kongnamul Guk is one of the staple soups of Korea, traditionally made with soybean sprouts. You can taste very little difference when you use more nutritious mung bean sprouts. The flavor of this soup, which is usually served as a side dish, is rich, slightly salty and deliciously crunchy. It's great for balancing out the flavors and soothing your tongue and stomach when you are eating a spicy main dish.

Serves 4

8 oz (227 g) mung bean sprouts (about 4 cups)

6 cups (1.5 L) water

¼ cup (7.5 g) dried anchovies

2 cloves garlic, thinly sliced

1 tsp saewoojeot

½ tsp sea salt

½ tsp gochugaru, or more to taste

1 green onion, chopped

Cauliflower Sticky Rice (page 182), for serving

Kimchi, for serving

Wash the mung bean sprouts under cold running water, then drain and set aside.

Add the water and dried anchovies to a large pot and heat over medium-high heat. Cover and bring to a boil. Reduce the heat to medium-low and simmer for 15 minutes. Remove the anchovies and discard them.

Increase the heat to medium-high, then add the mung bean sprouts to the pot. Cover, and let it boil for 5 minutes. Add the garlic, saewoojeot, sea salt, gochugaru and green onion, and let it boil for 2 minutes. Taste the soup and add more sea salt and/or gochugaru, if needed.

Remove from heat and serve as a side dish with Cauliflower Sticky Rice and kimchi.

Tip: If you can't find saewoojeot, substitute it with the same amount of fish sauce.

MAEUNTANG
(Spicy Fish Stew)

This seafood stew has many variations and can be made using all different kinds of fish. If you aren't comfortable cooking a whole fish, you can use one that's already filleted, but the taste will be compromised. There's something about using whole bone-in fish that creates a deep, nutritious flavor, and if you do have leftovers, you'll find that a properly made Maeuntang will gel once cooled, much like high-quality bone broth.

Serves 4

1 whole red snapper or cod

4 cups (1 L) water

3" (7.5-cm) piece dried kelp (also called dashima or kombu)

8 oz (227 g) daikon or Korean radish, cut into thin 1" (2.5-cm) squares

2 tbsp (30 ml) Gochujang (Korean Red Chili Paste) (page 174)

2 tbsp (30 ml) fish sauce

1 tsp gochugaru

2 red or green chili peppers, sliced

2 cloves garlic, minced

1" (2.5-cm) piece fresh ginger, minced

4 oz (114 g) shrimp, deveined and heads removed

4 oz (114 g) clams

1 bunch of crown daisy (also called chrysanthemum or sukgat), cut into 2–3" (5–7.5-cm) pieces

2 green onions, cut into 2" (5-cm) pieces

1 bunch enoki mushrooms, ends cut and separated

Cauliflower Sticky Rice (page 182), for serving

Clean the fish by washing it under cold water. Scale the fish, if needed, and cut off the fins. Cut the fish into 3-inch (7.5-cm) pieces and reserve the head. Set aside in the refrigerator.

In a large pot, combine the water and kelp. Bring the water to a boil over high heat, then reduce the heat to medium and simmer for 10 minutes. Remove and discard the kelp.

Add the radish slices, Gochujang, fish sauce, gochugaru, chili peppers, garlic and ginger. Cover and cook for 5 minutes.

Add the shrimp, fish head and fish pieces, cover and let them simmer for 7 to 8 minutes. Add the clams and cook for 5 minutes until they open up. Add the crown daisy, green onions and enoki mushrooms and simmer for 3 minutes, until the vegetables are just cooked through.

If you don't want to serve the fish head, remove and discard it before serving. Serve hot with a side of Cauliflower Sticky Rice.

Tip: If you have difficulty finding crown daisy, substitute it with 1 bunch of spinach.

GOOKSOO TIME!

(Noodles)

GookSoo, or noodles, are enjoyed in various forms in Korea, and noodle dishes are considered a quick meal because you can slurp them down fast. Although they can be enjoyed any time of the year, long noodles symbolize long life, so they are frequently eaten on birthdays and during the Lunar New Year celebration.

There are so many varieties of gooksoo, and they are served hot, cold, sweet, salty, spicy, in soups, stir-fries and more. You'll find some of the most popular noodle dishes (which happen to be my favorites as well) in the next several pages, like Bibim Naengmyun (Spicy Cold Noodles) (page 82), Jjajangmyun (Noodles in Black "Soybean" Sauce) (page 86) and Japchae (Stir-Fried Sweet Potato Noodles) (page 89).

SPICY KOREAN RAMEN

When Koreans eat ramen, it comes in an instant package 99 percent of the time. It's a seriously delicious junk food that is hard to resist, especially because it's so cheap and easy. I was appalled the first time I read the ingredients list on a typical ramen package, and I haven't touched them since. This healthy veggie-packed version doesn't contain any of the junk, but tastes pretty dang close to the real stuff.

Serves 4

10 cups (2.5 L) water

⅓ cup (10 g) dried anchovies

6" (15-cm) piece kelp (also called dashima or kombu)

1 large onion, quartered

4 cloves garlic, whole

1 lb (454 g) beef brisket, cut into 2" (5-cm) pieces

4 eggs

4 medium white-fleshed sweet potatoes, peeled

1 tbsp (15 ml) cooking oil, plus more if needed

12 shiitake mushrooms, sliced

2 cloves garlic, minced

1 cup (150 g) kimchi, drained and cut into bite-sized pieces

½ cup (120 ml) kimchi juice

2 tbsp (30 ml) coconut aminos

1 tbsp (15 ml) Gochujang (Korean Red Chili Paste) (page 174)

2 tsp (5 g) gochugaru

1 tsp onion powder

1 tsp sea salt

2 green onions, sliced thinly

In a large pot, combine the water, dried anchovies and kelp. Bring to a boil over high heat, then reduce the heat to medium-low and simmer for 5 minutes. Remove the kelp from the broth, then let it simmer for 15 minutes. Use a fine mesh strainer to remove the anchovies and discard them.

Increase the heat to high, then add the onion, 4 cloves garlic and the beef brisket to the pot. Let it come to a boil. Cover, reduce the heat to medium-low and let the meat simmer for 40 minutes, or until tender.

Add the eggs to the pot of beef and vegetables and let them simmer for 7 minutes. Prepare a large bowl with an ice bath while the eggs are simmering. Remove the eggs, then immediately place them in the ice bath.

Turn off the heat, transfer the beef to a bowl and strain and discard the vegetables from the broth. Use 2 forks to shred the beef into bite-sized pieces. Once cool enough to handle, peel the eggs and set aside. Return the pot of broth to the stovetop over low heat and cover until ready to use.

Use a spiralizer or a vegetable peeler to slice the sweet potatoes into noodles. Set aside.

Heat the cooking oil over medium-high heat in a skillet. Add the mushrooms and cook, stirring, for 3 minutes until they are browned. Add more oil, if needed, then add the shredded beef. Cook, stirring, until the beef pieces are crisped up, about 5 minutes. Remove from the heat.

Uncover the pot of broth and increase the heat to high. Add the minced garlic, kimchi, kimchi juice, coconut aminos, Gochujang, gochugaru, onion powder and sea salt. Once everything comes to a boil, decrease the heat to medium-low and simmer for 5 minutes, then add in the spiralized sweet potatoes. Let it simmer for 3 minutes.

Divide the broth and its contents among 4 bowls. Top each bowl with the mushroom, beef mixture and sliced green onions. Carefully slice the eggs in half and add 2 halves to each bowl. Serve immediately.

BIBIM NAENGMYUN
(Spicy Cold Noodles)

This is a cold dish enjoyed in the summer, and it's probably my favorite Korean noodle recipe. I like to make a double batch of the spicy, tangy sauce and use it as hot sauce on, well, pretty much anything. Usually, Bibim Naengmyun uses buckwheat noodles and then radish slices as one of the toppings, but I decided to make noodles with the actual radish, which turned out even more refreshing than the original version.

Serves 4

1 lb (454 g) beef brisket

8 cups (2 L) water

2 lb (908 g) daikon radish

1 tbsp (15 ml) apple cider vinegar

½ tsp sea salt

2 eggs

Spicy Sauce

½ cup (120 ml) reserved beef broth

2 tbsp (30 ml) Gochujang
(Korean Red Chili Paste) (page 174)

2 tbsp (30 ml) apple cider vinegar

2 tbsp (30 ml) coconut aminos

1 tsp (3 g) gochugaru, or more to taste

1 tbsp (8 g) toasted sesame seeds

2 tsp (10 ml) sesame oil

½ tsp sea salt

½ Asian pear, roughly chopped

¼ medium onion

2 cloves garlic

½ Asian pear, julienned

1 English cucumber, julienned

Place the beef brisket in a large pot and cover it with the water. Heat over high heat and once it comes to a boil, cover the pot and reduce the heat to medium-low. Simmer for 1 hour until the brisket is tender, adding more water if needed. Remove the brisket and reserve the broth. Let the brisket cool, then cut into thin slices.

Use a spiralizer or a vegetable peeler to slice the daikon radish into noodles. Bring the beef broth from the previous step to a boil over high heat in the same pot. Add the daikon noodles and boil for 3 minutes. Transfer the daikon noodles to a mesh strainer and run under cold water for 2 to 3 minutes. Shake off any excess water and transfer to a bowl. Add the apple cider vinegar and sea salt. Mix well, and set aside. Reserve ½ cup (120 ml) of broth.

Fill up a separate saucepan with water and bring to boil over high heat. Lower the whole eggs into the broth gently so they don't break, and let it come to a boil again. Once it does, bring down the heat to medium-low and let the eggs simmer for 11 minutes. Prepare a large bowl with an ice bath. Once the eggs are done cooking, place them in the ice bath for at least 10 minutes. Peel the eggs under cold running water. Cut each egg in half.

For the spicy sauce, combine ½ cup (120 ml) of the reserved beef broth, the Gochujang, vinegar, coconut aminos, gochugaru, sesame seeds, sesame oil, salt, ½ Asian pear, onion and garlic in a blender or a food processor. Blend until smooth. Taste and add more gochugaru for a spicier sauce.

To assemble your Bibim Naengmyun bowls, divide the daikon noodles into 4 bowls, and add the spicy sauce evenly over the noodles. Divide the sliced beef, ½ Asian pear, cucumber and hard-boiled eggs over the noodles. Serve immediately. Mix everything well before eating!

MUL NAENGMYUN

(Cold Broth Noodles)

During the humid summers in Korea, popular cold noodle restaurants are hoppin' with lines out the door. There's nothing that cools you down better than a bowl of Mul Naengmyun, with its icy cold broth to wash down every bite. While it is a bit labor-intensive, everything can be made ahead of time, so make a big batch and enjoy it for days.

Serves 4

Beef Broth

1 lb (454 g) beef brisket

12 cups (3 L) water

4 oz (114 g) Korean or daikon radish

1 onion, peeled and quartered

2 green onions

3" (7.5-cm) piece kelp
(also called dashima or kombu)

6 cloves garlic, peeled and smashed

1" (2.5-cm) piece fresh ginger

8 black peppercorns

4 medium zucchini, spiralized

1 tbsp (15 ml) coconut aminos

1 tbsp (12.5 g) coconut sugar

2 tbsp (30 ml) apple cider vinegar or rice vinegar

1¼ tsp (7.5 g) sea salt, divided

2 eggs

1 kirby or pickling cucumber, halved lengthwise and thinly sliced

Thinly sliced radish from Dongchimi (Radish Water Kimchi) (page 113) or some Musaengchae (Sweet and Sour Radish Salad) (page 125)

1 small Asian pear, quartered, cored and thinly sliced

Toasted sesame seeds, for garnish

Mustard oil or hot mustard

Apple cider vinegar or rice vinegar

For the beef broth, combine the beef brisket, water, radish, onion, green onions, kelp, garlic, ginger and peppercorns in a large pot and bring to a boil over high heat. Reduce the heat to medium-low and simmer for 5 minutes. Remove and discard the kelp. Cover and continue to simmer for 1 to 1½ hours, or until the beef is cooked through and tender.

Remove the beef and transfer to the refrigerator. Drain and reserve the broth, and discard the vegetables. Place the broth back in the pot and let it come to a boil again over medium-high heat. Add the spiralized zucchini and let it simmer for 3 minutes. Remove the zucchini noodles and transfer to the refrigerator. Stir the coconut aminos, coconut sugar, vinegar and 1 teaspoon of sea salt into the broth. Taste to adjust seasoning. Let the broth cool for 10 minutes, then place it in the freezer for 3 hours.

While the broth chills, hard boil the eggs. Bring approximately 3 cups (720 ml) of water to a boil over high heat in a saucepan. Lower the eggs into the water gently so they don't break, and let it come to a boil again. Once it does, bring down the heat to medium-low and let the eggs simmer for 11 minutes. Prepare a large bowl with an ice bath. Once the eggs are done cooking, place them in the ice bath for at least 10 minutes. Peel the eggs under cold running water. Cut each egg in half and refrigerate until ready to serve.

Sprinkle the sliced cucumber with ¼ teaspoon of sea salt, mix well and let it sit for at least 15 minutes, until the slices are softened and wilted. Refrigerate until ready to serve.

To serve Mul Naengmyun, thinly slice the beef brisket. Take out the broth from the freezer. It should have a thin layer of ice on the top. Break this layer with a spoon or a knife so you have slushy chunks of ice floating. Divide the chilled zucchini noodles into 4 bowls. Top with the beef, cucumber, radish and pear slices. Add half an egg to each bowl, then pour the cold broth around the zucchini noodles. Sprinkle with toasted sesame seeds and serve with a side of mustard oil (or hot mustard) and vinegar.

JJAJANGMYUN
(Noodles in Black "Soybean" Sauce)

This is probably most Koreans' favorite Chinese–Korean dish. The sweet and salty dark sauce is made with black soybean paste, and it's easy to make quite a mess while eating this as a kid (or an adult, if you are like me). This grain-free version omits the soybean paste, but I was able to recreate the same umami flavor with a combination of real food ingredients. There are newer versions of jjajangmyun that use rice instead of noodles, so feel free to try the sauce with my Cauliflower Sticky Rice (page 182). The optional squid ink is added just to achieve the dark color of the original dish, but you can still fully enjoy the flavors without it.

Serves 6

6 medium zucchini

2½ tsp (15 g) sea salt, divided

1 lb (454 g) pork loin, cut into ½" (12-mm) cubes

¼ tsp ground black pepper

2 tbsp (30 ml) cooking oil, divided

1 medium onion, diced

1 medium potato, cut into ¼" (6-mm) cubes

2 carrots, cut into ¼" (6-mm) pieces

2 cloves garlic, minced

2¼ cups (540 ml) water, divided

¼ cup (60 ml) apple cider vinegar or coconut vinegar

2 tbsp (30 ml) coconut aminos

2 tbsp (30 ml) blackstrap molasses

1 tbsp (12.5 g) coconut sugar

1 tbsp (15 ml) fish sauce

1 tbsp (15 ml) tomato paste

3 tbsp (29 g) potato starch

¼ tsp squid ink, optional

1 medium cucumber, julienned, for serving

Danmuji (Sweet Pickled Radish) (page 109) rounds, for serving

Use a spiralizer or a vegetable peeler to slice the zucchini into noodles. Place zucchini noodles in a colander over a bowl, and toss with 1 teaspoon of sea salt. Let this sit for 30 minutes to sweat the zucchini. Drain and wrap the zucchini in a paper towel and squeeze out the moisture with your hands. Set aside.

Sprinkle the pork loin cubes with ½ teaspoon of sea salt and ground black pepper and mix thoroughly. Heat 1 tablespoon (15 ml) of cooking oil in a deep skillet over medium-high heat. Add the pork and stir-fry for 3 minutes until browned on the outside and halfway cooked.

Add the onion, potato, carrots and garlic to the skillet, and cook, stirring, for 4 to 5 minutes, until the onions turn translucent. While the vegetables are cooking, combine 2 cups (480 ml) of water, the vinegar, coconut aminos, blackstrap molasses, coconut sugar, fish sauce, tomato paste and 1 teaspoon of sea salt. Stir until evenly mixed. Pour this over the vegetables and increase the heat to high until everything comes to a boil. Reduce the heat to medium, and let the mixture simmer uncovered for 10 minutes, stirring frequently, until the potatoes can easily be pierced with a fork and the sauce is slightly reduced.

Whisk together the potato starch with ¼ cup (60 ml) of water to make a slurry. Slowly pour in the slurry over the meat and vegetables and stir. If using, stir in the squid ink at this time as well. Simmer, uncovered, for about 5 additional minutes until the sauce is thickened. Take off the heat and cover.

Heat 1 tablespoon (15 ml) of cooking oil in a separate skillet over medium-high heat. Add the zucchini noodles and cook, stirring, for 2 to 3 minutes, or until tender.

To serve, divide the zucchini noodles into 4 bowls. Add the sauce over the noodles, and top with the julienned cucumber. Serve with Danmuji rounds.

JAPCHAE
(Stir-Fried Sweet Potato Noodles)

Japchae is probably the only noodle recipe in which you don't need to substitute the noodles with spiralized vegetables to make it Paleo. It's made with chewy and light sweet potato starch noodles, called dangmyeon, which you can easily find at an Asian grocery store. Japchae is guaranteed to be served at any celebratory holiday, and it's packed with all the colorful vegetables and beef, tossed in a subtly salty and sweet marinade.

Serves 4

Marinade
6 tbsp (90 ml) coconut aminos

2 tbsp (30 ml) sesame oil

2 tsp (10 ml) maple syrup

2 tsp (10 ml) fish sauce

2 tsp (5 g) toasted sesame seeds, plus more for garnish

½ tsp ground black pepper

2 cloves garlic, minced

8 oz (227 g) beef sirloin or ribeye

4 shiitake mushrooms, stems removed

5–6 oz (142–170 g) fresh spinach

1 tsp sesame oil

¼ tsp sea salt, plus more to taste

6 oz (170 g) sweet potato starch noodles (also called dangmyeon)

5 tsp (25 ml) cooking oil, divided

1 large egg, beaten

1 onion, sliced

½ red bell pepper, cut into thin strips

1 carrot, julienned

2 green onions, cut into 1" (2.5-cm) pieces

For the marinade, combine the coconut aminos, sesame oil, maple syrup, fish sauce, sesame seeds, black pepper and garlic in a bowl, and mix until well combined.

Cut the beef into bite-sized strips and the shiitake mushrooms into thin slices. Combine the beef and mushrooms in a bowl. Add 2 tablespoons (30 ml) of marinade to the beef and mushrooms and mix. Set aside.

Bring a large pot of water to a boil over high heat. Add the spinach leaves and blanch for 30 seconds. Drain and rinse the spinach in a colander under cold water for 1 minute. Squeeze the spinach with your hands to get rid of any excess water. Add the sesame oil and sea salt and mix. Set aside.

Bring another large pot of water to a boil over high heat. Add the sweet potato starch noodles and boil for 5 to 7 minutes, according to the package directions. Drain and run the noodles under cold water for 1 minute. Cut the noodles 2 to 3 times. Place them in a bowl and mix with 1 tablespoon (15 ml) of the marinade. Set aside.

Heat 1 teaspoon of cooking oil in a large skillet over medium-low heat. Add the beaten egg and let it spread out in a thin layer. Cook for 2 minutes until the edges firm up. Flip the egg and cook for 2 more minutes. Transfer to a cutting board and let it cool. Cut into thin slices that are 2 to 3 inches (5 to 7.5 cm) long. Set aside.

Heat 2 teaspoons (10 ml) of cooking oil in the same skillet over medium-high heat. Add the onion, red bell pepper and carrot. Stir-fry for 2 to 3 minutes. Add the green onions and cook for 1 minute. Transfer the vegetables to the same bowl as the noodles.

Heat 2 teaspoons (10 ml) of cooking oil in the same skillet over medium-high heat. Add the beef and mushroom mixture and stir-fry for 3 to 4 minutes, until the meat is browned and the mushrooms are tender.

Reduce the heat to low and add the bowl of noodles and vegetables back into the skillet. Cook, stirring, for 1 minute. Turn off the heat and add the spinach, egg strips and the rest of the marinade. Stir well. Add more salt, if needed. Sprinkle with more toasted sesame seeds, and serve warm or at room temperature.

NOT-YOUR-TYPICAL PANCAKES

You won't find sweet, breakfast stacks when it comes to Korean cooking. Instead, there are crispy and savory pan-fried pancakes packed with vegetables and best served with a giant vat of makgeolli, or Korean rice wine. They are my absolute favorite Korean food, and it makes me giddy that I can enjoy the taste of them again with my Paleo versions.

Koreans often eat these pancakes when it's raining, and I'm actually unclear as to why. One theory I've read is that the sound of the rainfall reminds them of the sizzling sound of the pancake batter frying in oil, so they immediately start craving pancakes. Whatever the real reason, it's a tradition that's embedded in the culture, and it's a fun excuse to whip up some delicious savory pancakes on a rainy day!

HOBAKJEON
(Zucchini Pancakes)

Hobakjeon is a great way to fit in some nutritious veggies for kids because it's so crispy and tasty without an upfront taste of zucchini. It's simple and easy, and it can be made for a quick snack or as a full meal.

Serves 2

2 cups (350 g) julienned zucchini (about 1 large or 2 small)

1 tsp sea salt

½ cup (61 g) cassava flour

1 egg

2 tbsp (30 ml) cooking oil, for frying

Sweet and Sour Dipping Sauce (page 184), for serving

Toss the julienned zucchini with the sea salt in a bowl. Let it sit for 15 to 20 minutes. Use a cheesecloth or a nut milk bag to squeeze out as much liquid as you can from the zucchini, and reserve and set aside the liquid.

Place the zucchini in a mixing bowl and add the cassava flour, egg and ½ cup (120 ml) of zucchini liquid. Mix with a fork. If the batter seems too thick, add more zucchini liquid (1 tablespoon [15 ml] at a time) until it reaches the consistency of pancake batter. If you run out of the liquid, use plain water.

Heat your choice of cooking oil in a large skillet over medium-high heat. Wait 5 minutes until the pan gets very hot. Add the entire batter if you want to make 1 large pancake, or you can add a few tablespoons (30 to 60 ml) at a time to make several smaller pancakes. Let it cook for 1 minute, and then reduce the heat to medium and cook for an additional 1 to 2 minutes, until browned and crispy on the bottom. Flip and cook the other side for another 2 minutes, adding more oil if needed.

Serve immediately with a side of Sweet and Sour Dipping Sauce. You can cut the pancakes in smaller pieces, or rip them apart as you eat.

KIMCHI BUCHIMGAE

(Kimchi Pancakes)

This spicy, savory pancake is one of my favorites, and you can really taste the crunchy texture of kimchi in every bite. If you have old kimchi in the fridge that's gone fully sour, Kimchi Buchimgae is a great way to use it up.

Serves 3

1 cup (122 g) cassava flour

¼ cup (30 g) tapioca starch

½ tsp sea salt

1 egg

1 cup (240 ml) cold water

½ cup (120 ml) kimchi juice

1½ cups (225 g) well-fermented and sour kimchi, sliced thinly

⅓ medium onion, sliced thinly

2 green onions, chopped

3 tbsp (45 ml) cooking oil, for frying, divided

Sweet and Sour Dipping Sauce (page 184), for serving

In a large bowl, combine the cassava flour, tapioca starch and sea salt. Whisk together the egg, cold water and kimchi juice in a separate bowl. Pour the egg mixture into the flour mixture and mix well. Stir in the kimchi, onion and green onions.

Heat 1 tablespoon (15 ml) of oil in a large skillet over medium-high heat. Pour ⅓ of the pancake batter into the skillet and spread it out thinly with a spatula into an even layer. Let it cook for 4 to 5 minutes, until the bottom is crispy and browned. Carefully flip the pancake and cook the other side for 3 to 4 minutes until browned. Remove from the heat. Repeat 2 more times with the rest of the batter so you have 3 pancakes.

Serve immediately with a side of Sweet and Sour Dipping Sauce. You can cut the pancakes in smaller pieces, or rip them apart as you eat.

BUCHUJEON

(Garlic Chive Pancakes)

The thing I love the most about Buchujeon is that there's a much higher vegetables-to-flour ratio than other Korean pancakes. Because of this, this pancake works better if you make several smaller pancakes than 2 or 3 large ones, which may be more difficult to flip and hold together. It's a great way to fit in a lot of greens in a delicious way!

Serves 2-3

1 cup (122 g) cassava flour

1 tbsp (7 g) coconut flour

½ tsp sea salt

2¼ cups (540 ml) cold water

5 oz (142 g) garlic chives, chopped into 2" (5-cm) pieces

¼ medium onion, thinly sliced

1–2 serrano or jalapeño peppers, thinly sliced, optional

Cooking oil, for frying

Sweet and Sour Dipping Sauce (page 184), for serving

In a large bowl, combine the cassava flour, coconut flour and sea salt. Add the water and stir until a batter forms. Stir in the garlic chives, onion and peppers and mix well. It may look like you need more batter, but this is a veggie-heavy pancake!

Heat 1 tablespoon (15 ml) of oil in a large skillet over medium-high heat. Pour in a small amount of batter and spread it out with a spatula until you have a pancake about 4 inches (10 cm) wide. Fit in more pancakes in the same skillet if you can without them touching each other. Cook for 2 to 3 minutes, until the edges turn golden brown. Flip over the pancakes, adding more oil if necessary, and cook the other side for 2 minutes before removing from the skillet. Repeat with the rest of the batter.

Serve immediately with Sweet and Sour Dipping Sauce.

GAMJAJEON
(Potato Pancakes)

Gamjajeon is pure comfort food with its crispy exterior coating and velvety inside. If you make it the right way, you don't need to use any type of flour, but it's hard to find that when you order at a typical Korean restaurant. However, you can easily make it at home by following these simple steps, and it's hard not to fall in love with this humble dish.

Serves 2-3

1 lb (454 g) potatoes

½ medium onion

2 cloves garlic, peeled

Cooking oil, for frying

Sweet and Sour Dipping Sauce (page 184), for serving

Chop the potatoes and onion into chunks. Place the potatoes, onion and garlic in a blender and blend until smooth and creamy. Pour the blended mixture over a fine-mesh strainer placed over a bowl and let sit for 5 minutes. The liquid from the mixture should drip down into the bowl. Press down on the potato mixture lightly with a spatula a few times to help with the draining process.

Transfer the blended potato mixture to a large bowl. Pour out and discard the drained liquid from the potatoes slowly until you are left with the white, thick potato starch resting at the bottom. Add the starch back into the blended potato mixture and mix well.

Heat 1 tablespoon (15 ml) of cooking oil in a nonstick skillet over medium-high heat. Pour in 3 to 4 tablespoons (45 to 60 ml) of the potato mixture and spread it out in a 3- to 4-inch (7.5- to 10-cm) pancake. Add as many pancakes as you can fit on the pan. Reduce the heat to medium and let them cook for 2 minutes, until the bottom turns golden brown and crispy, pressing down lightly with a spatula. Flip the pancakes and cook for an additional 2 minutes. Repeat with the rest of the potato mixture.

Remove from the pan and serve immediately with Sweet and Sour Dipping Sauce.

HAEMUL PAJEON

(Seafood Pancakes)

This may be my favorite type of Korean pancake. The soft chewiness of the squid and shrimp complement the crispy dough so well, and couple that with the crunchiness of the green onions for a bite of heaven. While other pancakes are served as sides, Haemul Pajeon is often a full meal to accompany your makgeolli (Korean rice wine) or soju.

Serves 4

¾ cup (91.5 g) cassava flour

¼ cup (38 g) potato starch

½ tsp sea salt

1 egg

1 cup (240 ml) cold water

4 oz (114 g) peeled and deveined shrimp, diced

4 oz (114 g) squid, diced

1 clove garlic, minced

2 tbsp (30 ml) or more cooking oil, for frying, divided

8 green onions, halved lengthwise

2 red chili peppers, thinly sliced

Sweet and Sour Dipping Sauce (page 184), for serving

In a large bowl, combine the cassava flour, potato starch and sea salt. Add the egg and cold water and mix until a batter is formed. Stir in the shrimp, squid and garlic.

Heat 1 tablespoon (15 ml) of oil in a skillet over medium-high heat. If needed, cut the green onions so all the slices can fit inside the skillet you are using. Place half of the green onion slices on the pan in a single layer. Add ½ of the batter over the green onions, tilting the pan to spread it out in a circle. Place half of the red chili pepper slices evenly over the batter.

Turn down the heat to medium and let the batter fry for about 4 minutes, then carefully flip the pancake, adding more oil if needed. Cook for an additional 3 to 4 minutes until cooked through. Repeat with the other half of batter and ingredients.

Serve with Sweet and Sour Dipping Sauce.

MORE BANCHAN PLEASE?

(Side Dishes)

Banchan in Korean refers to small side dishes, and you've probably tried them if you've ever dined at a Korean restaurant. They usually come with your meal and are served as soon as you sit down. In a typical everyday meal, each person is served a bowl of rice, and several banchan dishes are laid out in the middle to share, along with a main protein dish and/or some kind of stew. Because you eat them with rice, most banchan are flavored a bit saltier and spicier than if you would eat them by themselves.

I don't give serving sizes in this chapter because the amount of banchan you eat in one meal varies depending on how much you enjoy it and if there are other banchan dishes on the table you like more than others. They are served in small plates and are replenished in the same meal, if needed. The number of banchan laid out is always different, depending on how fancy the meal is and how much the cook has prepared. If they are super yummy, I'm happy with just two or three for a simple meal at home.

KKAKDUGI

(Radish Kimchi)

While cabbage kimchi is the OG of the Korean food scene, Kkakdugi is my favorite type of kimchi because of its crunchy, refreshing texture. It's actually easier to make than cabbage kimchi, but it's packed with the same amount of gut-loving probiotics.

Yields about 8 cups (1350 g)

3 lb (1.3 kg) Korean or daikon radish

1 tbsp + 1 tsp (24 g) sea salt

5 cloves garlic, minced

1" (2.5-cm) piece ginger, finely grated

⅓ cup (80 ml) fish sauce

⅓ cup (43 g) gochugaru

4 green onions, chopped

Rinse the radish and cut off any small hairs on the skin. You can also peel the skin, but I like to leave it on. Cut the radish into bite-sized cubes and put them in a large mixing bowl. Coat the mixture evenly with sea salt and let it rest for 30 minutes so the cubes have time to sweat.

Drain out the juice. Add the garlic, ginger, fish sauce, gochugaru and green onions. Mix everything well so the spices are evenly coated. Taste and add more gochugaru or fish sauce, if needed.

Transfer to a glass jar with an airtight lid, pressing down the mixture gently as you pour it in. Close the lid and let it sit at room temperature out of sunlight for 24 to 48 hours while it ferments.

It's ready when you open the lid and you see small bubbles escaping off the top and the kkakdugi has a strong, sour smell. Store in the fridge and eat it with everything! It will keep well for longer than a year, but you may want to eat it within 3 to 4 months before it gets way too sour.

SIGEUMCHI NAMUL

(Spinach Salad)

I love Sigeumchi Namul because it really shows the amount of healthy nutrients you can pack into one dish. A large amount of spinach is cooked down to just a fraction of its original volume so you can fit in a ton of greens in one sitting. So much more nutritious than a regular raw salad!

Yields about 1 cup (180 g)

10–12 oz (283–340 g) fresh spinach

1 green onion, thinly sliced

1 tbsp (15 ml) coconut aminos

1 tsp apple cider vinegar or coconut vinegar

1 tsp sesame oil

1 tsp toasted sesame seeds

1 clove garlic, minced

Bring a large pot of water to a boil over high heat. Add the spinach leaves and blanch for 30 seconds. Drain and rinse the spinach in a colander under cold water for 1 minute. Squeeze the spinach with your hands to get rid of any excess water and place in a bowl.

Add the green onion, coconut aminos, vinegar, sesame oil, sesame seeds and garlic and toss until well combined. Let the mixture sit for 15 minutes until the flavors meld and build. Serve immediately or store in the refrigerator for 3 to 4 days.

DANMUJI
(Sweet Pickled Radish)

While not commonly used as banchan, Danmuji is a must-have when it comes to certain dishes like Classic Bulgogi Kimbap (Korean Sushi) (page 15) and Jjajangmyun (Noodles in Black "Soybean" Sauce) (page 86). You'll recognize it for its distinctive yellow color derived from turmeric, and its sweet and sour flavor makes it easy to eat a lot of.

Yields 5-6 cups (900 g)

2 lb (908 g) daikon radish, peeled

1½ cups (360 ml) filtered water, plus more as needed

1½ cups (360 ml) apple cider vinegar or coconut vinegar

¾ cup (150 g) coconut sugar

1 tbsp (18 g) sea salt

1 tsp turmeric powder

10 black peppercorns

Slice the daikon radish into rounds, or cut them into ¼-inch (6-mm) strips. I like to do half of each. Rounds are used as banchan to eat alongside other dishes, and strips are used to make Classic Bulgogi Kimbap (Korean Sushi) (page 15).

In a saucepan, combine the water, vinegar, coconut sugar, salt, turmeric powder and peppercorns. Heat over medium-high heat until it comes to a boil. Stir until the coconut sugar is fully dissolved, then remove from the heat.

Add the daikon radish to the saucepan and let it cool to room temperature. Transfer the contents to a glass jar or container with an airtight lid. Add more water if the brine doesn't cover the radish all the way.

Screw on the lid and let it sit out at room temperature for 12 to 24 hours. The color of the radish will turn deep yellow. Transfer it to the refrigerator. The pickled radish keeps for up to a month.

DUBU BUCHIM

(Pan-Fried Tofu with "Soy" Garlic Sauce)

There's something about crispy fried tofu that I just can't get enough of. Pair that with a delicious garlic sauce and it can be the star of a meal on its own. If you want an extra easy way to enjoy pan-fried tofu, you can just top it with a piece of kimchi instead of making the sauce. Try it out if you don't believe me!

Yields 30–40 tofu pieces

1 batch Hemp Tofu (page 181)

2 tbsp (30 ml) cooking oil

"Soy" Garlic Sauce
3 tbsp (45 ml) coconut aminos

1 tsp gochugaru

½ tsp sesame oil

1 tsp toasted sesame seeds

¼ tsp ground black pepper

¼ tsp maple syrup

1 green onion, thinly sliced

If previously made and stored in water, pat the Hemp Tofu dry with a paper towel. Quarter the tofu block, then slice each quarter into rectangular pieces about ¼ inch (6 mm) thick.

Heat the cooking oil in a large skillet over medium-low heat. Once fully heated, pan fry the tofu slices for 5 minutes per side, until crispy and golden brown. Transfer the tofu to a serving dish.

Make the "Soy" Garlic Sauce by mixing the coconut aminos, gochugaru, sesame oil, sesame seeds, black pepper, maple syrup and green onion together in a bowl. Evenly drizzle the sauce over the tofu slices. Serve warm.

DONGCHIMI

(Radish Water Kimchi)

If you don't like spicy kimchi, you may want to try out Dongchimi. It is just as tangy and refreshing without the heat, and the dongchimi water is delicious enough to drink on its own. The hot peppers are used to subtly flavor the liquid and aren't meant to be eaten, so don't be afraid to use them.

Yields about 16 cups (4 L)

2 lb (908 g) Korean or daikon radish

½ napa cabbage

¼ cup (60 g) sea salt

1 ripe Asian pear

6 cups (1.5 L) water, divided

8 cloves garlic, smashed and peeled

2 green onions, sliced into 2" (5-cm) pieces

2 red or green hot peppers

Thoroughly wash the radish and napa cabbage. Cut the radish into wedges about 2 inches (5 cm) long and ½ inch (12 mm) wide. Cut the napa cabbage in half again lengthwise, then remove the core. Cut each quarter crosswise into 2- to 3-inch (5- to 7.5-cm) pieces.

Combine the radish and cabbage slices in a large bowl and sprinkle with sea salt. Use your hands to massage the salt in evenly. Let this mixture sit at room temperature for at least 2 hours until softened and wilted, and about ½ cup (120 ml) of liquid sweats out. Do not drain the liquid.

Quarter and core the pear. Cut it into small chunks and place in the blender. Add 1 cup (240 ml) of water, then blend until smooth. Strain the pear liquid through a cheesecloth or nut pulp bag, squeezing out all the pear juice. Discard the pulp.

Add the garlic, green onions and hot peppers to the salted radish and cabbage. Pour in the pear juice and 5 cups (1.3 L) of water. Stir well.

Transfer to a clean glass container with an airtight lid. Let it sit at room temperature out of sunlight for up to 2 days. The water will turn cloudy and bubbly as it ferments. Transfer to the refrigerator. You can eat it right away or let it ferment for 2 more weeks in the refrigerator until it gets even tangier and more refreshing. Serve as a side dish. Store it in the refrigerator and eat it within 2 to 3 months.

GAJI NAMUL
(Steamed Eggplant Salad)

If you are an eggplant lover, you'll love Gaji Namul. It's steamed to tender perfection while still being slightly crunchy, then coated in flavorful dressing, resulting in a delicious banchan to eat with rice.

Yields 5 cups (454 g)

1 lb (454 g) Asian/Korean eggplants (about 2 large or 3 medium)

2 cups (480 ml) water

2 green onions, chopped

2 tbsp (30 ml) coconut aminos

2 tsp (10 ml) sesame oil

2 tsp (10 ml) apple cider vinegar or coconut vinegar

½ tsp fish sauce

2 cloves garlic, minced

1 tsp toasted sesame seeds

¼ tsp gochugaru

Cauliflower Sticky Rice (page 182), for serving

Cut the eggplants crosswise into 3 to 4 equal pieces, depending on their lengths. Then slice each piece lengthwise into quarters.

Prepare a steamer by filling the base with the water, then let it come to a boil over medium-high heat. Add the eggplants to the steamer basket and steam for 4 minutes, until tender. Transfer the eggplants to a large bowl and let them cool for 10 minutes.

Add the green onions, coconut aminos, sesame oil, vinegar, fish sauce, garlic, sesame seeds and gochugaru to the eggplants and toss until well combined. Let the mixture sit for 10 to 15 minutes so the flavors can meld. Serve with Cauliflower Sticky Rice. You can serve the leftovers cold and eat it within 3 to 4 days.

GYERANMARI
(Rolled Omelet)

Gyeranmari literally translates to "rolled egg," and this dish is exactly that. A thin layer of egg is rolled up with various vegetables, then sliced into bite-sized pieces. It's a popular lunch box recipe because it transports so well.

Yields 12 omelet slices

3 eggs

¼ tsp sea salt

⅛ tsp ground black pepper

2 tbsp (12.5 g) finely chopped green onions

2 tbsp (19 g) finely chopped red bell pepper

1 tbsp (8 g) finely chopped carrot

2 tsp (10 ml) coconut oil

4–5 pieces of Gim Gui (Roasted Seaweed) (page 129), optional

Cauliflower Sticky Rice (page 182), for serving

Whisk together the eggs, sea salt and ground black pepper until the stringy egg whites are mixed in. Add the green onions, red bell pepper and carrot. Whisk again.

Heat the coconut oil in a 10- to 12-inch (25- to 30-cm) skillet over medium-low heat. Tilt the pan to make sure the coconut oil covers the entire pan, and wait 4 to 5 minutes to make sure the pan is fully heated.

Pour the whisked egg mixture into the skillet and spread it out. Let it cook for 2 minutes, until the eggs start to set at the bottom but are still uncooked at the top. If using, lay down 4 to 5 pieces of Gim Gui on top, covering about ¾ of the eggs. Let the eggs cook for 1 to 2 more minutes, or until almost set but still moist at the top.

Using a wide spatula, lift and fold over 1 to 2 inches (2.5 to 5 cm) of the omelet on the side opposite where you laid down the Gim Gui. Flatten the folded part of the egg with your spatula, then lift up that fold and fold again. Repeat this process until all the eggs are rolled up. Let it cook on the pan for 30 more seconds, then flip and cook the other side for 30 seconds.

Remove from the heat and transfer to a plate or a cutting board. Let it sit for 5 minutes. Carefully cut the Gyeranmari into ½-inch (12-mm) slices. Serve immediately with Cauliflower Sticky Rice or eat it on its own.

JANGJORIM
("Soy" Braised Beef and Eggs)

While typically served as a side dish, I like to cook this up and enjoy it as the main dish. Growing up, I used to love the eggs that become flavored and colored with the braising soy liquid, and I remember asking for a much higher egg-to-beef ratio when my mom would make JangJoRim. It's still my favorite part!

Yields 6 cups (454 g)

5 cups (1.3 L) water

3 green onions, cut in half

¾ cup (180 ml) coconut aminos

2 tbsp (30 ml) apple cider vinegar or coconut vinegar

1 tsp honey

1 tsp sea salt

1 lb (454 g) beef brisket, cut into 2" (5-cm) chunks

1 cup (90 g) shishito peppers

10 cloves garlic

4 eggs

Cauliflower Sticky Rice (page 182), for serving

Combine the water, green onions, coconut aminos, vinegar, honey and sea salt in a large pot and heat on the stovetop over high heat. Let it come to a boil, then add the beef brisket chunks. Cover, lower the heat to medium, then let the meat boil for 40 minutes or until tender. You should be able to pierce the meat easily with a fork.

Add the shishito peppers, garlic cloves and whole eggs to the pot, then add more water if needed. Cover and boil for 10 minutes.

Turn off the heat, then discard the green onions. Remove the brisket and eggs, and run the eggs under cold water until cool enough to handle. Tear the brisket into bite-sized pieces and peel the eggs. Add them back into the pot, and let the whole thing cool completely.

Transfer the shishito peppers, garlic cloves, brisket and eggs to a large container, and pour the broth over them until they are submerged. Discard the leftover broth, or save it to flavor other dishes. Store the JangJoRim in the refrigerator. Once chilled, the fat will turn white, harden and float to the top. Gently remove and discard the fat with a spoon.

JangJoRim can be served chilled, at room temperature or hot. Slice the eggs before serving with the meat and vegetables. Enjoy it with Cauliflower Sticky Rice. It'll last in the refrigerator for up to a week.

GYERAN JJIM

(Steamed Egg Pot)

If you own a microwave, Gyeran Jjim may be the easiest recipe to make, but don't let the simple instructions fool you. This side dish is packed with flavor, and you'll fall in love with its velvety texture. It's one of the most popular banchans you can find at Korean restaurants.

Yields 1½ cups (243 g)

4 eggs

¾ cup (180 ml) water

2 tsp (10 ml) fish sauce

1 green onion, chopped

½ tsp sesame oil

Ground black pepper, for garnish, optional

Microwave Method

Whisk together the eggs, water and fish sauce until well combined. Stir in the chopped green onion.

Grease a large microwaveable bowl with sesame oil. Pour the whisked egg mixture into the bowl. Make sure you leave at least 1 inch (2.5 cm) of room from the top.

Microwave for 5 minutes, until the eggs are fluffy and cooked through. Sprinkle with ground black pepper, if using, and serve hot.

Stovetop Method

Whisk together the eggs, water and fish sauce until well combined. Stir in the chopped green onion.

Grease a heavy-bottomed pot with sesame oil, and pour in the whisked egg mixture. Make sure you leave at least 1 inch (2.5 cm) of room from the top.

Heat the pot over medium-high heat until the eggs start to boil. Turn the heat down to low, cover and let it cook for 3 minutes. Uncover and stir the eggs for even cooking, then cover and simmer for an additional 5 minutes, until cooked through.

Sprinkle with ground black pepper, if using, and serve hot.

MIYEOK MUCHIM

(Seaweed Salad)

Miyeok Muchim is different from the typical Japanese seaweed salad you may be used to. It uses a different kind of seaweed that's thicker and darker with a less "crunchy" texture. It's hard not to eat a lot of this sour and tangy cold salad, especially on a hot summer day.

Yields 4 cups (144 g)

1 oz (28 g) dried seaweed (also called mareun miyeok or wakame)

Dressing
¼ cup (60 ml) apple cider vinegar or coconut vinegar

2 tsp (10 ml) coconut aminos

1 tsp honey

½ tsp sea salt

2 cloves garlic, minced

½ tsp gochugaru, optional

1 cup (116 g) julienned or shredded Korean or daikon radish

¼ medium onion, sliced thinly

1 tsp toasted sesame seeds, for garnish

Place the seaweed in a large bowl and pour water over it until it's completely submerged. Let it sit at room temperature for 30 minutes until rehydrated to about 3 cups (480 ml), then drain.

Bring a large pot of water to a boil over high heat. Boil the seaweed in the water for 1 minute. Drain and rinse the seaweed thoroughly under cold water in a fine-mesh strainer. Squeeze out the excess water with your hands, then cut the seaweed into 2-inch (5-cm) pieces.

For the dressing, mix the vinegar, coconut aminos, honey, sea salt, garlic and gochugaru, if using, in a large bowl. Add the seaweed, radish and onion to the dressing. Toss well to combine. Sprinkle with the toasted sesame seeds and serve cold. It'll keep well in the refrigerator for up to a week.

MUSAENGCHAE

(Sweet and Sour Radish Salad)

Musaengchae is not only delicious on its own, it's also used in dishes like Mul Naengmyun (Cold Broth Noodles) (page 85) and Bossam (Pork Belly Wraps) (page 47). It's one of the dishes that gets better and better the longer it sits, so I like to make a big batch and eat it for a few days as a quick and easy side dish.

Yields 3 cups (227 g)

8 oz (227 g) Korean or daikon radish

1 clove garlic, minced

2 green onions, chopped

1–2 tbsp (15–30 ml) apple cider vinegar or coconut vinegar

1 tsp coconut sugar

¼ tsp sea salt

½ tsp gochugaru, or more, optional

Peel the radish and julienne it to thin matchsticks. Place in a bowl and add the minced garlic and green onions.

In a separate bowl, combine 1 tablespoon (15 ml) of vinegar, the coconut sugar, sea salt and gochugaru, if using, until the salt and coconut sugar are mostly dissolved. Pour this over the vegetables and mix well. Taste the radish to adjust the seasoning, adding more vinegar if needed.

Chill for at least 20 minutes before serving. The flavors will build more as it sits and taste even better the next day. Store in the refrigerator for up to a week.

SUKJU NAMUL

(Mung Bean Sprout Salad)

While mung beans aren't 100 percent Paleo, sprouted beans are in the gray area because they are so nutritious and the sprouting process reduces their anti-nutrient effect. I actually feel really great eating sprouted beans, when I usually have issues with regular beans, so feel free to experiment to see if it's right for you. Sukju Namul is one of those must-have banchan items in a Korean meal, so I highly recommend you try it out!

Yields 2 cups (454 g)

1 lb (454 g) fresh mung bean sprouts

1 green onion, thinly sliced

2 tsp (10 ml) sesame oil

1 tsp toasted sesame seeds

1 tsp minced garlic

1 tsp sea salt

Bring a large pot of water to a boil over high heat. Add the mung bean sprouts and boil for 2 minutes. Transfer the sprouts to a large colander and run them under cold water for 2 minutes.

Squeeze the sprouts with your hands to get rid of any excess water. Place them in a large mixing bowl.

Add the green onion, sesame oil, sesame seeds, garlic and sea salt and toss until well combined. Serve immediately or store in the refrigerator for 3 to 4 days.

GIM GUI
(Roasted Seaweed)

Gim Gui is one of those snacks and side dishes that have gotten extremely popular in recent years, and I see it prepackaged at all health food grocery stores. While many of them are cooked in inflammatory oils, you may be surprised to learn that it is extremely easy and fun to make at home at a fraction of the price and in a healthier way. If you are eating it as banchan, wrap a little bit of rice in it for a quick and simple sushi roll.

Yields 120-180 seaweed pieces

1 tbsp (15 ml) avocado oil

1 tbsp (15 ml) sesame oil

20 sheets of dry unseasoned seaweed (also called gim or nori)

Sea salt

Mix the avocado oil and sesame oil in a small bowl. Lay the seaweed sheets flat with the shiny side up. Use a pastry brush or your hands to gently brush the oil mixture on the shiny side so you cover the entire sheet with a thin layer. Sprinkle lightly with a pinch of sea salt. Repeat with the rest of the nori sheets, stacking them as you go so both sides get flavored with sea salt.

Heat a large skillet over medium-high heat. Place a seaweed sheet on the skillet and toast for 5 to 10 seconds, until it shrinks and turns slightly green. Flip and toast the other side for a similar amount of time. Repeat with the rest of the seaweed sheets.

Use kitchen shears to cut the toasted seaweed sheets into 6 or 8 equal rectangles. Enjoy immediately, or store them in an airtight container at room temperature for 3 days or in the freezer for up to 3 months.

MANEUL JJANGACHI

(Pickled Fermented Garlic)

While Maneul Jjangachi may sound a bit odd to those who aren't used to the concept, it's a side dish that's loved by many in Korea. The fermentation process tones down the strong and spicy garlic taste, but I can't guarantee that you won't have garlic breath after eating a couple of these. In my opinion, it's totally worth it, especially for its amazing health benefits. I like to load up on Maneul Jjangachi when I feel like I'm coming down with something: it's an instant immune system booster!

Yields 4½ cups (454 g)

1 lb (454 g) fresh garlic (about 10 heads)

1⅓ cups (320 ml) apple cider vinegar, divided

Water

¾ cup (180 ml) coconut aminos

2 tbsp (30 ml) honey

Separate the garlic cloves from the heads and cut off the root ends. Place in a large bowl and cover with hot water for 30 minutes to 1 hour so they are easier to peel. Peel the skin, then drain. Place the peeled garlic in a 1-quart (1-L) glass jar.

Add 1 cup (240 ml) of apple cider vinegar, then fill the rest with water until the garlic cloves are completely submerged. Close the lid and let it sit at room temperature for a week.

Drain the liquid from the jar. Combine the coconut aminos, ⅓ cup (80 ml) of apple cider vinegar and honey, then pour it into the jar with the garlic cloves. If the garlic cloves aren't completely covered by the brine, add water until they are.

Let the jar sit at room temperature for 2 weeks or longer. I've let them ferment for over a month. The longer they sit, the better the flavors will build. Begin tasting weekly, and once they have fermented to your liking, transfer to the refrigerator. They will last indefinitely.

OI SOBAGI
(Stuffed Cucumber Kimchi)

Another one of my favorite dishes growing up, Oi Sobagi is a popular summer kimchi in which cucumbers are stuffed with a spicy sauce made with various vegetables and seasonings. It's one of the crunchiest kimchi varieties after Kkakdugi, and you'll love the refreshingly cooling flavors that awaken your taste buds.

Yields about 4 cups (454 g)

1 lb (454 g) pickling or kirby cucumbers

1 tbsp (18 g) sea salt

Kimchi Sauce

4 oz (114 g) garlic chives (also called buchu), cut into ½" (12-mm) pieces

½ small onion, thinly sliced

½ cup (58 g) grated or shredded daikon radish

3 cloves garlic, minced

1" (2.5-cm) piece fresh ginger, minced

¼ cup (32 g) gochugaru

2 tbsp (30 ml) water

1 tbsp (15 ml) fish sauce

1 tbsp (18 g) saewoojeot, or substitute sea salt

1 tsp coconut sugar

Wash the cucumbers, then slice them lengthwise, leaving about ½ inch (12 mm) of one end uncut. Slice the cucumbers again in the same way, but this time perpendicular to the first cut so you have 2 cuts on each cucumber that look like an "X" from one end.

Place the cucumbers in a bowl and sprinkle evenly with sea salt, rubbing it both inside and outside of the cucumbers. Let this sit for 30 minutes, then wash the cucumbers to remove all the salt.

For the kimchi sauce, combine the garlic chives, onion, radish, garlic, ginger, gochugaru, water, fish sauce, saewoojeot and coconut sugar in a stainless steel or glass bowl until a thick, clumpy paste forms. Stuff the sauce inside the cucumbers and cover the outside as well, being careful not to break the uncut ends.

Transfer the stuffed cucumbers into a clean airtight glass container, cover and let sit at room temperature for 24 hours so it can ferment and the flavors can meld together. Store in the refrigerator for up to a week and serve cold.

BEST OF BOTH WORLDS
(Fusion)

I had so much fun creating these Paleo fusion dishes, and I loved that I was able to flex my creative muscles to combine my favorite flavors and ingredients. If you are intimidated about cooking Korean food for the first time, start here so you can tread on familiar territory and slowly transition to other recipes in this book.

From Spicy Kimchi Chicken Pizza (page 143) to Gochujang Shrimp Tacos (page 139) to Bulgogi Burger (page 148), you'll find a way to enjoy distinct Korean flavors in popular dishes you know so well.

PULLED PORK WITH KOREAN BBQ SAUCE

This pulled pork topped with Gochujang-based BBQ sauce is deliciously spicy, tangy and slightly sweet at the same time. Enjoy it in Korean Pulled Pork Sweet Potato Nachos (page 147) or any way that you'd normally eat pulled pork. It also freezes well, making it a great batch cooking recipe.

Serves 8-10

4-5 lb (1.7-2.2 kg) boneless pork shoulder/butt

1 tbsp (18 g) sea salt

1 tbsp (12.5 g) coconut sugar

1 tsp gochugaru

¼ tsp ground cinnamon

1 tbsp (15 ml) cooking oil

2 large onions, sliced

5 cloves garlic, peeled and minced

½ cup (120 ml) chicken stock

Korean BBQ Sauce

½ cup (120 ml) Gochujang (Korean Red Chili Paste) (page 174)

½ cup (120 ml) coconut aminos

¼ cup (60 ml) tomato paste

¼ cup (60 ml) water

½ cup (120 ml) apple cider vinegar or coconut vinegar

2 tbsp (30 ml) sesame oil

2 tbsp (30 ml) honey

2 tsp (4.5 g) garlic powder

2 tsp (4.5 g) onion powder

Cut the pork in half. In a small bowl, combine the sea salt, coconut sugar, gochugaru and ground cinnamon and mix well. Sprinkle and rub the spice mix all over the pork evenly.

Slow Cooker Method

For the slow cooker, heat the cooking oil in a large skillet over medium heat. Working in batches if needed, add the pork in a single layer and brown on all sides, about 5 minutes.

Add the onions, garlic and chicken stock to the slow cooker. Lay the pork on top and cook on low for 8 to 10 hours, until tender and cooked through.

For the Korean BBQ sauce, add the Gochujang, coconut aminos, tomato paste, water, vinegar, sesame oil, honey, garlic powder and onion powder to a saucepan. Cook, stirring, over low heat for 5 minutes until well combined and warmed through.

Once done cooking, transfer the pork and onions to a large plate using a slotted spoon. Discard the juice in the slow cooker. Use 2 forks to shred the pork into bite-sized pieces. Return the shredded pork to the slow cooker.

Spoon the Korean BBQ sauce over the meat. Serve immediately or cook on low until ready to serve.

(continued)

Instant Pot Method

Set the Instant Pot to "Sauté" and heat the cooking oil inside the pot. Wait until the Instant Pot signals that it's hot; then sear the pork in batches until the meat is browned on all sides, about 5 minutes. Turn off the Instant Pot and remove the pork.

Add the onions, garlic cloves and chicken stock to the Instant Pot and stir. Lay the pork on top, then close the lid and make sure the pressure valve is sealed. Set the Instant Pot to manual pressure on high for 90 minutes. Once done cooking, let it sit for 10 to 15 minutes until the pressure naturally releases.

For the Korean BBQ sauce, add the Gochujang, coconut aminos, tomato paste, water, vinegar, sesame oil, honey, garlic powder and onion powder to a saucepan. Heat, stirring, over low heat for 5 minutes until well combined and warmed through.

Once the Instant Pot pressure is fully released, transfer the pork and onions to a large plate using a slotted spoon. Discard the juice in the Instant Pot. Use 2 forks to shred the pork into bite-sized pieces. Return the shredded pork to the Instant Pot.

Spoon the Korean BBQ sauce over the meat. Serve immediately or set the Instant Pot to "warm" until ready to serve.

GOCHUJANG SHRIMP TACOS

Shrimp tacos are my favorite kind of tacos, and this Gochujang-flavored version does not disappoint. What really makes this dish is the avocado-pineapple salsa that's bursting with tangy flavor and complements the meaty shrimp perfectly.

Serves 3

Gochujang Shrimp

2 tbsp (30 ml) Gochujang (Korean Red Chili Paste) (page 174)

1 tbsp (15 ml) coconut aminos

1 tbsp (15 ml) apple cider vinegar or coconut vinegar

1 tsp sesame oil

1 lb (454 g) peeled and deveined shrimp

1 tbsp (15 ml) cooking oil

Toasted sesame seeds, for garnish

Avocado-Pineapple Salsa

1 large avocado, seeded and peeled

⅔ cup (150 g) drained pineapple chunks, fresh or canned

1 red or green jalapeño pepper, seeds and membranes removed

¼ cup (40 g) chopped onions

2 tbsp (2 g) chopped cilantro leaves

1 green onion, chopped

2 tbsp (30 ml) lime juice

1 tbsp (15 ml) coconut aminos

1 tbsp (15 ml) sesame oil

2 tsp (8 g) coconut sugar

¼ tsp gochugaru

1 clove garlic, peeled and minced

Gochujang Shrimp

In a bowl, whisk together the Gochujang, coconut aminos, vinegar and sesame oil. Place the shrimp in a resealable bag or a glass container. Pour the Gochujang sauce over the shrimp and massage to coat. Transfer to the refrigerator and marinate for 1 hour to overnight.

When it's time to cook the shrimp, make the Avocado-Pineapple Salsa and the Grain-Free Tortillas (recipe to follow) first.

Heat the cooking oil in a skillet over medium-high heat. Shake off the marinade from the shrimp and lay the shrimp in a single layer on the skillet, discarding the marinade. Work in batches if you need to so you don't crowd the pan. Cook for 2 minutes, then flip and cook for 2 additional minutes. Remove from the heat. Sprinkle with the toasted sesame seeds.

Avocado-Pineapple Salsa

Dice the avocado and pineapple chunks into small cubes and chop the jalapeño pepper. Combine in a large bowl with the onions, cilantro leaves and green onion. In a separate bowl, whisk together the lime juice, coconut aminos, sesame oil, coconut sugar, gochugaru and garlic. Pour this dressing over the avocado and pineapple mixture. Toss to combine. Refrigerate until ready to use.

(continued)

Grain-Free Tortillas

¾ cup (91.5 g) cassava flour

¼ cup (30 g) tapioca starch

¼ tsp sea salt

¾ cup (180 ml) hot water

2 tbsp (30 ml) sesame oil

1 tsp honey

Grain-Free Tortillas

In a large bowl, mix together the cassava flour, tapioca starch and sea salt. In a separate bowl, whisk together the hot water, sesame oil and honey. Slowly pour the wet ingredients into the dry ingredients, whisking continuously. The mixture should form a dough, and you may not need to use all the liquid.

Shape the dough into 6 balls. Dust a rolling pin and the surface you are working on liberally with cassava flour. Use the rolling pin to roll out each ball into a thin circle about 6 to 7 inches (15 to 18 cm) in diameter, adding more cassava flour as you go to keep the tortilla from sticking.

Heat a dry skillet over medium-high heat. Place a tortilla on the skillet and let it heat up for 45 seconds. Flip and repeat for 45 seconds. The tortillas should look slightly charred and golden. Repeat with the rest of the tortillas, stacking the finished tortillas with a kitchen towel or a paper towel between each layer. Keep them warm while the shrimp cooks by wrapping the whole thing with a dry kitchen towel.

To assemble the tacos, divide the cooked shrimp and lay them down on top of the tortillas. Top with Avocado–Pineapple Salsa. Serve immediately.

SPICY KIMCHI CHICKEN PIZZA

Pizza is extremely popular in Korea, and there are so many interesting variations you can find there. This is my take on bringing my favorite foods together, and this crispy potato pizza crust holds up surprisingly well. You can play around with different vegetables and toppings if you don't have all the ingredients on hand!

Serves 4

Potato Pizza Crust

1½ lbs (681 g) russet potatoes (about 2 large or 3 medium), peeled and cut into chunks

1 cup (96 g) blanched almond flour

1 egg

1 tsp sea salt

1 tsp garlic powder

Kimchi Cashew Cheese

⅔ cup (82 g) raw cashews, soaked for at least 4 hours

¼ cup (60 ml) kimchi juice

3 tbsp (45 ml) extra virgin olive oil

2 tbsp (30 g) nutritional yeast

1 tbsp (15 ml) coconut aminos

½ tsp sea salt

2 cloves garlic

Toppings

2 green onions, cut into 1–2" (2.5–5-cm) pieces

½ red bell pepper, sliced thinly

½ cup kimchi, drained and chopped

1½ cups (360 g) chopped Dakkochi (Spicy Chicken BBQ Skewers) (page 39)

Gochujang Mayonnaise (page 151)

Chopped cilantro, garlic powder, toasted sesame seeds and/or gochugaru, for garnish, optional

Before you begin, make sure your cashews for the Kimchi Cashew Cheese have soaked for at least 4 hours. Prepare the topping ingredients.

Combine the raw potato chunks and almond flour in a food processor and blend until creamy. Add the egg, sea salt and garlic powder, and pulse several times. Mix with a spatula. It'll feel like a thick paste. Place in the refrigerator for 20 minutes. It may turn a bit brown, but that's okay.

Preheat the oven to 400°F (204°C). Line a baking sheet with parchment paper. Remove the dough from the fridge, pour it out onto the parchment paper and flatten it out with a spatula into a crust that's about ¼ to ½ inch (6 to 12 mm) thick. The dough may seem wet, but it'll firm up while baking. You can make 1 large pizza or 2 smaller pizzas. Bake for 35 minutes.

For the kimchi cashew cheese, while the crust is baking, place the cashews, kimchi juice, olive oil, nutritional yeast, coconut aminos, sea salt and garlic in a blender and blend until smooth and creamy.

Once the dough has finished baking, spread on the kimchi cashew cheese. Add a layer of green onions, red bell pepper and kimchi. Top with Dakkochi. Place back in the oven for 10 minutes until the veggies are cooked and the crust is golden brown.

Drizzle with Gochujang Mayonnaise and top with optional garnishes before serving.

BACON KIMCHI FRIES

Well, there's just no way you can go wrong with this recipe, is there? Crispy oven-baked fries are topped with kimchi pan-fried in bacon fat, creating the most addictive combo of flavors and textures. Whether it's for a group or just yourself, I'd be surprised if there are any leftovers.

Serves 4

Oven-Baked Fries

3 medium russet potatoes (about 1½ lbs [681 g])

1 tbsp (15 ml) avocado oil or olive oil

1 tsp sea salt

Bacon Kimchi Toppings

4 slices thick-cut bacon, chopped

½ medium onion, thinly sliced

2 cloves garlic, minced

1 cup (150 g) drained well-fermented kimchi, chopped

1 green onion, chopped, for garnish

Toasted sesame seeds, for garnish

¼ cup (60 ml) Gochujang Mayonnaise (page 151)

Scrub the potatoes under running water. Cut the potatoes into thin wedges about ¼ inch (6 mm) wide. Soak the potato wedges in water for at least 30 minutes.

Preheat the oven to 450°F (232°C). Line a baking sheet with parchment paper, or place a wire rack over a baking sheet. Drain and rinse the potatoes, then lay them on a kitchen towel or paper towels. Blot the tops to dry them as much as you can.

Place the potatoes in a large bowl and toss them with the oil and sea salt, making sure all slices are coated well. Spread the potatoes in a single layer on the parchment paper or wire rack without overlapping or crowding the pan. Use 2 pans if you need to. Bake for 30 minutes, flipping the fries halfway through if you are cooking on parchment paper, until golden brown. Turn the pan at the 15-minute mark to ensure even cooking.

While the fries are baking, prepare the toppings. Heat a large skillet over medium heat on the stovetop. Add the bacon and cook, stirring, until browned and crispy, about 5 minutes. Remove the bacon with a slotted spoon and set aside.

Increase the heat to medium-high. In the same skillet with the bacon fat, add the onion, garlic and kimchi. Stir-fry for 5 to 6 minutes, until the kimchi is browned and caramelized.

Place the fries in a serving dish. Top with the cooked kimchi, then the crispy bacon. Sprinkle with chopped green onion and toasted sesame seeds, then drizzle with Gochujang Mayonnaise.

KOREAN PULLED PORK SWEET POTATO NACHOS

When someone asks me what my last meal would be, my immediate answer is, "nachos with ALL THE TOPPINGS." That's how much I love nachos, and these Korean Pulled Pork Sweet Potato Nachos are one of the best I've had. There are so many flavors and textures that work so well together, and the sweet potato chips do a great job of staying crispy and strong enough to hold up all the delicious toppings.

Serves 4

Sweet Potato Chips
1½ lbs (681 g) sweet potatoes (about 3 medium)

1–2 tbsp (15–30 ml) sesame oil

Pinch of sea salt

Nachos
1 tbsp (15 ml) cooking oil

2 cups (500 g) Pulled Pork with Korean BBQ Sauce (page 137)

½ cup (74 g) Musaengchae (Sweet and Sour Radish Salad) (page 125)

¼ red onion, diced

¼ cup (22.5 g) fresh or pickled sliced jalapeños

½ avocado, diced

Juice from ¼ lime

⅓ cup (80 ml) Gochujang Mayonnaise (page 151)

Chopped green onions and cilantro, for garnish

Sweet Potato Chips
Preheat the oven to 325°F (163°C), and move 2 oven racks to the center. Use a mandolin or a sharp knife to slice the sweet potatoes as thinly as possible. Place the sweet potato slices in a large bowl and cover them with water for 15 minutes.

Drain off the water and pat the potato slices dry with a paper towel. Lightly brush each potato slice with sesame oil front and back. Line 2 baking sheets with parchment paper. Place the potato slices on the parchment paper in a single layer without overlapping. Use more baking sheets if needed. Sprinkle sea salt evenly over the sweet potatoes.

Bake the sweet potato slices on the 2 center racks for 20 minutes. Rotate the pans, switch racks and bake for another 20 minutes. Check on the chips. Some of the chips may have curled up and started browning and crisping up. Remove the crispy ones from the oven and set aside. They'll crisp up more while cooling.

Keep baking the rest of the chips and check up on them every 5 minutes to remove the ones that have crisped up. Let them cool completely once all the chips are finished cooking.

To prepare the nachos, heat the cooking oil in a large skillet over medium-high heat. Add the Pulled Pork with Korean BBQ Sauce and stir-fry for 5 minutes until the meat is crispy and heated through. Remove from the heat.

On a large platter, spread out the sweet potato chips in an even layer. Add a layer of pork, then a layer of Musaengchae (Sweet and Sour Radish Salad). Add the red onion, jalapeños and avocado pieces. Drizzle the whole thing with the lime juice and Gochujang Mayonnaise. Garnish with green onions and cilantro. Serve immediately.

BULGOGI BURGER

This is a popular fusion recipe that can be found at more and more restaurants, and with so many variations. The bulgogi flavor on the burger works so well and the crunchy, tangy toppings elevate it even more. I hope my flavor bomb version achieves the double duty of fulfilling your cravings for a burger and Korean food at the same time.

Serves 3

Cabbage Slaw

1 cup (90 g) thinly sliced napa cabbage or regular cabbage

2 tbsp (30 ml) Gochujang Mayonnaise (page 151)

1 tsp apple cider vinegar or coconut vinegar

Bulgogi Burger

1 lb (454 g) ground beef

1 green onion, finely chopped

1" (2.5-cm) piece ginger, minced

1 clove garlic, minced

1 tbsp (15 ml) coconut aminos

2 tsp (8 g) coconut sugar

½ tsp sea salt

¼ tsp ground black pepper

Portobello Buns

6 portobello mushrooms, stems removed

2 tbsp (30 ml) cooking oil

Salt and pepper, to taste

Toppings

Danmuji (Sweet Pickled Radish) rounds (page 109)

Cilantro leaves, for garnish

Gochujang Mayonnaise (page 151)

For the cabbage slaw, combine the cabbage, Gochujang Mayonnaise and vinegar. Place in the refrigerator until ready to use.

For the burger, place the ground beef, green onion, ginger, garlic, coconut aminos, coconut sugar, sea salt and black pepper in a bowl and mix. Form into 3 burger patties that are ½ inch (12 mm) thick. Make an indent with your thumb at the center of each burger.

Heat the grill over medium-high heat. Brush the portobello mushrooms on both sides with oil. Lightly sprinkle with salt and pepper. Place on the preheated grill, cover and grill for 5 minutes on each side. Pour out any liquid that may have cooked out on the caps and set aside.

Place the burgers on the grill. Cook, covered, for 4 to 6 minutes per side, depending on your preference of doneness. Let the burgers rest for 5 minutes.

Assemble the burgers. Place a patty on top of a portobello cap, then layer with Danmuji, cabbage slaw and cilantro. Drizzle with Gochujang Mayonnaise, then finish with another portobello cap. Repeat with the rest of the burgers. Serve immediately.

Tip: Don't have a grill? You can panfry the burgers and the portobello mushrooms in a skillet over medium-high heat for the same amount of time.

KIMCHI DEVILED EGGS

This recipe puts a fun twist on everyone's favorite appetizer or snack by adding a bit of spice to the classic deviled eggs. The chopped kimchi adds a nice, refreshing crunch surprise in the creamy filling. You'll see these disappear in minutes at parties!

Serves 6

Gochujang Mayonnaise
2 eggs

1 cup (240 ml) avocado oil

¼ cup (60 ml) apple cider vinegar

2 tsp (10 ml) Dijon mustard

½ tsp honey

3 tbsp (45 ml) Gochujang
(Korean Red Chili Paste) (page 174)

Kimchi Deviled Eggs
6 eggs

3 tbsp (45 ml) Gochujang Mayonnaise

1 tbsp (15 ml) kimchi juice

⅓ cup (50 g) kimchi, drained and finely chopped

¼ tsp toasted sesame oil

Sea salt, to taste

Toasted sesame seeds and finely chopped green onions, for garnish

Gochujang Mayonnaise
In a wide-mouthed glass jar that can fit the head of the immersion blender, add the eggs, avocado oil, apple cider vinegar, Dijon mustard and honey. Slowly lower the blender into the jar until it hits the bottom. Turn on the blender and let it run without moving until you see a white creamy cloud start forming from the bottom. It will rise up as the oil gets slowly incorporated into the mixture. When most of the oil is blended into a creamy mixture, about 10 seconds, slowly lift the blender up while it's running. By the time you get to the top, there shouldn't be much oil left and your mayonnaise should be ready.

Add the Gochujang to the mayonnaise and stir until combined. Taste, and add more Gochujang if you want it spicier. Chill to thicken, and store.

Kimchi Deviled Eggs
Bring a saucepan of water to a boil over high heat. Take out the eggs straight from the refrigerator, then lower the eggs into the water gently so they don't break. Let the water come to a boil again. Once it does, lower the heat to medium-low, and let the eggs simmer for 11 minutes.

Prepare a large bowl with an ice bath while the eggs are cooking. Once the eggs are done, place them in the ice bath for at least 10 minutes. Peel the eggs under cold running water, then slice them in half lengthwise. Take out the yolks and place them in a large bowl.

Add the Gochujang Mayonnaise, kimchi juice, chopped kimchi and toasted sesame oil to the bowl. Use a fork to mash and mix everything together until creamy. Taste and add sea salt, if needed.

Fill the egg whites with the mixture evenly. Sprinkle with toasted sesame seeds and chopped green onions before serving.

SOMETHING SWEET TO BALANCE OUT THE SPICY

Unlike in the United States, Korean desserts aren't typically eaten after meals, and they are actually reserved for holidays like the Lunar New Year or Chuseok (Korean Thanksgiving). While this has been changing as the country has become more Westernized, traditional treats like Gang Jeong (Sesame Candy) (page 156), YakGwa (Honey Cookies) (page 159) and Goguma Mattang (Caramelized Sweet Potatoes) (page 168) are still mostly eaten on special occasions.

I've also included some modern snacks and desserts that are enjoyed more frequently, like Pepero (Chocolate-Covered Cookie Sticks) (page 160) and Kkwabaegi (Twisted Sugar Doughnuts) (page 163). All these recipes are a great way to #treatyoself and to soothe the palate after all the spicy Korean dishes you'll be trying out.

HODDEOK
(Sugar-Filled Pancakes)

Hoddeok is a popular street snack dessert in Korea, and this crispy fried dough stuffed with hot sugary filling is especially delicious in the winter. It always reminds me of my dad, who has a huge sweet tooth and would always buy these at rest stops when we would go on road trips when I was younger.

Serves 6

1 package (2½ tbsp [9 g]) active dry yeast

½ tsp sea salt

¾ cup (180 ml) warm water

¾ cup (95 g) tapioca starch

½ cup (61 g) cassava flour

½ cup (48 g) blanched almond flour

Sweet Filling
¼ cup (50 g) coconut sugar

½ tsp cinnamon

2 tbsp (15 g) crushed almonds, walnuts or pine nuts

Cooking oil, for frying

Whisk together the active dry yeast and sea salt in the warm water. Add the tapioca starch, cassava flour and almond flour and mix until a sticky dough forms. Cover the bowl with plastic wrap and let it sit for 1 hour at room temperature. The dough should rise and double in size. Knead the dough to get rid of air bubbles and let it sit for 10 minutes.

Make the sweet filling by mixing the coconut sugar, cinnamon and crushed nuts in a bowl.

Once the dough is ready, divide it into 6 equal pieces. Flatten out each piece, and place a tablespoon (11 g) of the sweet filling into the center before folding the edges and rolling it into a ball. You should have 6 dough balls with sweet filling centers.

Heat a tablespoon (15 ml) of oil in a skillet over medium heat and grease a spatula with the same cooking oil. Add a ball to the pan and slowly flatten it with a spatula until it's about 4 inches (10 cm) wide. Cook for about 1 to 2 minutes, until the bottom is browned. Flip and cook for 1 to 2 more minutes on the other side. Repeat with the rest of the dough balls, adding more oil as needed.

Let the Hoddeok cool for 5 minutes before serving. The sweet filling will be very hot.

GANG JEONG

(Sesame Candy)

This crunchy sesame seed candy, commonly served over traditional holidays, is quite addictive because it's deliciously nutty and not overly sweet. You can use already toasted sesame seeds, but I prefer to toast them before making the candy because the flavor is so much better that way. Make sure to work quickly when you roll out the sesame seed mixture. It's doesn't take long for it to harden into candy.

Serves about 16–18

2 cups (300 g) sesame seeds, white, black or both

1″ (2.5-cm) piece ginger, minced

½ cup (100 g) coconut sugar

½ cup (120 ml) honey

¼ tsp sea salt

If you are using raw sesame seeds, heat a large skillet over medium-low heat. Add the sesame seeds and toast them, stirring often, for 5 to 7 minutes, until fragrant. If you are using toasted sesame seeds, start at the next step.

Combine the toasted sesame seeds and minced ginger in a bowl, mixing well.

Prepare a baking sheet lined with parchment paper. Have another piece of parchment paper of a similar size ready.

Combine the coconut sugar, honey and sea salt in a small saucepan and heat over medium heat while constantly stirring. Once it comes to a full boil, let it cook for 2 minutes while stirring, then remove from the heat. Immediately pour the sesame seeds and ginger into the hot syrup and stir. Pour and spread this mixture on the parchment-lined baking sheet. Place the second piece of parchment paper on top of the mixture. Use a rolling pin to flatten the candy into an even thickness, about ¼ to ½ inch (6 to 12 mm).

Remove the top piece of parchment paper, and let it cool for 10 minutes. Use a sharp knife to cut the Gang Jeong into rectangles or squares.

Let it cool completely before storing in an airtight container. You can even freeze Gang Jeong for up to 3 months.

YAKGWA
(Honey Cookies)

This traditional cookie is usually shaped into a flower design, and it's common to see them on special celebrations and holidays. The dough is fried twice before getting coated in a layer of honey syrup, making it soft and chewy on the inside while crispy and sweet on the outside.

Serves about 25-30

Honey Syrup
½ cup (120 ml) water

1 cup (240 ml) honey

1" (2.5-cm) piece ginger, grated

¼ tsp cinnamon

3 cups (720 ml) coconut oil, avocado oil or palm shortening, for frying

1½ cups (183 g) cassava flour, plus more if needed

⅛ tsp sea salt

3 tbsp (45 ml) sesame oil

1 cup (240 ml) water, plus more if needed

3 tbsp (45 ml) honey

2 tbsp (30 ml) apple cider vinegar or coconut vinegar

2 tbsp (15 g) pine nuts, chopped

Make the honey syrup by combining the water, honey, ginger and cinnamon in a saucepan. Heat over medium heat until it comes to a boil, then reduce the heat to medium-low and simmer for 10 minutes. The mixture should thicken a bit. Take it off the heat and set aside.

Heat the oil in a saucepan over medium-low heat for 10 minutes until it reaches about 230 to 250°F (110 to 121°C).

While the oil is heating up, combine the cassava flour and sea salt in a mixing bowl. Add the sesame oil and mix well until combined. Combine the water, honey and vinegar in a separate bowl, then pour into the flour mixture. Mix with your hands until a dough is formed. If the dough feels too dry, add water 1 tablespoon (15 ml) at a time until it reaches the right consistency. If the dough is too wet, add a bit more cassava flour.

Dust your working surface with cassava flour. Roll out the dough with a rolling pin until it is about ¼ to ½ inch (6 to 12 mm) thick. Use a cookie mold of your choice, or use a knife to cut the dough into diamonds. Poke 3 or 4 holes in the center of each YakGwa with a toothpick to ensure even cooking.

Prepare a plate lined with paper towels. Working in batches, drop a few YakGwa into the heated oil without crowding the saucepan. They should sink immediately, then slowly float in a few minutes. Transfer them to the paper towel once they float to the top. Repeat with the rest of the YakGwa.

Raise the heat of the oil to medium-high, until it reaches 350°F (177°C). Working in batches, fry the YakGwa for the second time for about 1 minute, until they turn golden brown. Place them back on the paper towel to drain the oil a bit.

Work in batches to transfer the YakGwa into the honey syrup, coating them fully. Remove from the syrup and place them on parchment paper. Sprinkle with pine nuts.

Cool before serving, or store them in the refrigerator for up to a week.

PEPERO

(Chocolate-Covered Cookie Sticks)

Pepero is a Korean version of the Japanese Pocky sticks. They are essentially long, crispy cookie sticks that are coated in chocolate, and they were one of my favorite treats to beg for when we were at the store. The best thing about making these at home is that you can choose whatever toppings you like to coat the chocolate with.

Yields about 25-30 Pepero

Cookie Sticks

1 cup (96 g) blanched almond flour

¼ cup (32 g) arrowroot starch

½ tsp baking powder

¼ tsp sea salt

2 tbsp (30 ml) maple syrup

1 tbsp (15 ml) coconut oil, melted

½ tsp vanilla extract

Chocolate Layer

1 cup (180 g) semisweet chocolate chips

Shredded coconut, toasted sesame seeds, chopped nuts, chopped dried fruits, for topping, optional

Heat the oven to 350°F (177°C) and line a baking sheet with parchment paper.

In a large bowl, combine the almond flour, arrowroot starch, baking powder and sea salt and mix to combine. Add in the maple syrup, coconut oil and vanilla, and mix until a dough forms.

Using your hands, take a small portion of the dough and roll it on a wooden cutting board to create thin sticks, about 6 to 7 inches (15 to 18 cm) long and ⅛ to ¼ inch (3 to 6 mm) wide. Repeat with the rest of the dough, and lay them out on the baking sheet in a single layer, making sure they don't touch each other. You should end up with 25 to 30 cookie sticks.

Bake in the oven for 10 minutes until all the cookie sticks are golden brown, rotating the pan halfway through. Cool completely.

In a double boiler or in the microwave, heat the chocolate chips until they are completely melted. Let the chocolate cool for 10 minutes. The chocolate can break the cookie sticks if it is too hot. Take each cookie stick and use a spoon to brush on the chocolate all around, leaving about 1 inch (2.5 cm) of the stick uncovered on the bottom. If using, sprinkle with optional toppings. Place the cookie sticks back on the parchment paper until the chocolate has completely set, about 2 to 3 hours.

Store in an airtight container in the refrigerator for up to a week.

KKWABAEGI

(Twisted Sugar Doughnuts)

Throughout my short childhood in Korea, my mom worked at a bank that was next to a famous bakery. To treat us a couple times a week, she would bring home all kinds of delicious desserts from the bakery, and Kkwabaegi was a common choice. These deep-fried sugar doughnuts might actually be my dad's favorite, and something about the twisted shape makes them even more delectable.

Serves 8

1¼ cups (160 g) arrowroot powder, plus more for dusting

½ cup + 2 tbsp (70 g) coconut flour, plus more if needed

1 tsp psyllium husk

½ tsp baking soda

¼ tsp sea salt

¼ tsp cinnamon

2 large eggs

¾ cup (180 ml) full-fat coconut milk

¼ cup (60 ml) maple syrup

¼ cup (50 g) coconut sugar

½ tsp cinnamon

Refined coconut oil, palm shortening or avocado oil, for frying

In a large mixing bowl, combine the arrowroot powder, coconut flour, psyllium husk, baking soda, sea salt and cinnamon. In a separate bowl, whisk together the eggs, coconut milk and maple syrup. Add the wet ingredients to the dry ingredients and mix well to combine. Place the dough in the refrigerator for 5 minutes until the dough firms up. The dough should be slightly sticky but still be moldable. If the dough is too sticky to work with after letting it set, add 1 tablespoon (7 g) of coconut flour at a time, mix and wait 5 minutes until it gets to the right consistency.

Divide the dough into 8 equal pieces. Prepare a baking sheet with parchment paper. Dust some arrowroot starch on the surface you are working on. Take each piece of the dough and pass it from one hand to the other while smashing it, to get rid of air bubbles. Roll out the dough into a 12-inch (30-cm) rope about ½ to ¾ inch (12 to 18 mm) thick. Gently fold the rope in half without breaking it, and twist the halves of the rope together 3 or 4 times. Lightly push the ends together and lay it on the parchment paper. Repeat with the rest of the dough pieces until you have 8 twisted doughnuts lying on the parchment paper.

Prepare the cinnamon sugar coating by blending the coconut sugar and cinnamon in a blender or coffee grinder until powdery. Place in a bowl.

In a large saucepan or a deep skillet, heat 3 inches (7.5 cm) of coconut oil over medium-high heat until it reaches 350 to 360°F (177 to 182°C). Using a slotted spatula or spoon, gently drop the doughnuts into the oil. Work in batches to make sure the doughnuts are not crowded in the pan while they are cooking. Let them fry for 2 to 3 minutes while turning them every 30 seconds.

Once they are dark and golden, place the doughnuts back on the parchment paper and immediately sprinkle evenly all over with the cinnamon sugar coating. Repeat with the rest of the doughnuts, and serve immediately.

PATBINGSOO

("Red Bean" Shaved Ice)

This shaved ice treat is extremely popular in the summer, and there are so many cafés that specialize in it. The original version is made by topping a mound of shaved ice with sweet red beans, fruits, condensed sweet milk and grain powder. Sounds odd but it's actually a really yummy dessert, and I'm so happy to recreate it using purple sweet potato to substitute the flavor and texture of red beans.

Serves 2

1 small purple sweet potato (enough to yield about ½ cup [100 g] mashed)

2 tbsp (30 ml) maple syrup

¼ cup + 2 tbsp (90 ml) full-fat coconut milk, divided

1 tsp honey

3 cups (720 g) ice cubes

4 strawberries, sliced

¼ cup (82.5 g) chopped pineapple, fresh or canned

½ kiwi, chopped

½ banana, sliced

1 tsp maca powder, optional

Cook the sweet potato any way you like. I like to boil mine in water for 10 to 12 minutes, until it is easily pierced with a fork. Let it cool completely and peel the skin. Using a fork, mash the sweet potato with the maple syrup and 2 tablespoons (30 ml) of coconut milk.

Combine ¼ cup (60 ml) of coconut milk and the honey in a saucepan and heat over low heat until hot, but not boiling. Whisk together until the honey is fully dissolved. Chill in the refrigerator until ready to use.

Place the ice cubes in a food processor, and blend until they are the consistency of shaved ice. Divide the ice into 2 serving bowls. Freeze until ready to serve.

When ready to assemble, remove the shaved ice from the freezer. Divide the mashed sweet potato, strawberries, pineapple, kiwi and banana between the 2 bowls over the shaved ice. Drizzle the sweetened coconut milk over the toppings. If using, sprinkle each PatBingSoo with ½ teaspoon of maca powder before serving.

TWIGAK
(Sweet Fried Kelp Chips)

These kelp chips can also be categorized as a savory snack because they contain both sweet and salty flavors in one bite. I didn't really love the complex flavors of Twigak when I was younger, but my older brother would go crazy over them. I have now learned to appreciate this crunchy snack, and it's also a yummy way to get in some of the beneficial minerals and nutrients that are abundant in kelp.

Serves 4

2 sheets of kelp (also called dashima or kombu), about 6 x 12" (15 x 30 cm)

Avocado oil, for frying

1 tbsp + 2 tsp (18.5 g) coconut sugar

2 tsp (5 g) toasted sesame seeds

Using a slightly damp towel or a paper towel, gently wipe the kelp sheets front and back, concentrating on the areas with the white salt coating. Using kitchen shears, cut the kelp into 2-inch (5-cm) squares.

Heat 2 inches (5 cm) of avocado oil in a deep skillet over medium heat until the temperature reaches 300°F (149°C). Mix the coconut sugar and toasted sesame seeds together in a small bowl, and have a large mixing bowl ready. Add about a quarter of the kelp pieces to the oil. Because of the salt content of the kelp, you'll hear a crackling sound while frying, and the oil may splatter out, so be careful. Let the kelp pieces fry for about 10 seconds, until they are curled and their surfaces are bubbling, and they float to the top. Use a slotted spoon or a spider strainer to remove the kelp pieces to the mixing bowl, then immediately sprinkle them with a quarter of the coconut sugar and sesame seed mixture and toss. Repeat 3 more times with the rest of the kelp pieces and the sugar coating.

Once finished, let the TwiGak cool completely before enjoying. You can store these in an airtight container at room temperature for several days.

GOGUMA MATTANG
(Caramelized Sweet Potatoes)

This popular dessert is loved by many for its soft, fluffy inside that's covered by a sweet, crunchy layer. While it's traditionally deep-fried, this baked version still creates that addictive crispiness without the extra work.

Serves 4

1 lb (454 g) sweet potatoes, preferably Korean or Japanese

2 tbsp (15 g) tapioca starch

2 tbsp (30 ml) coconut oil, divided

¼ tsp sea salt

2 tbsp (25 g) coconut sugar

2 tbsp (30 ml) raw honey

Toasted sesame seeds, for garnish

Preheat the oven to 400°F (204°C) and line a large baking sheet with parchment paper.

Peel the sweet potatoes and cut them in half lengthwise, then cut them into 1- to 2-inch (2.5- to 5-cm) cubes, making sure they are all evenly sized. Place the sweet potatoes in a large bowl and toss them with the tapioca starch, making sure all the pieces are evenly coated. Pour this mixture into a mesh strainer and shake off the excess starch. Discard the leftover tapioca starch from the bowl.

Place the sweet potatoes back into the bowl and toss with 1 tablespoon (15 ml) of coconut oil and the sea salt until they are evenly coated. Transfer the sweet potatoes to the baking sheet in a single layer, making sure not to crowd the pan. Bake for 25 to 30 minutes, flipping the cubes halfway through. Remove from the oven and let the sweet potatoes cool.

Heat a skillet over medium heat and add 1 tablespoon (15 ml) of coconut oil, the coconut sugar and honey. Once this mixture begins to boil, turn the heat to low and simmer for 5 minutes. The coconut sugar should be dissolved at this point.

Turn off the heat and add the sweet potatoes to the skillet and stir to coat quickly. Lay the coated sweet potatoes back on the parchment paper, making sure they don't touch each other. Sprinkle with toasted sesame seeds. Cool for 10 minutes before serving.

KOREAN KITCHEN MUST-HAVES

Something I believed years ago but now realize to be completely untrue (and me just being lazy, of course) is this: Korean cooking is complicated, difficult and time-consuming. If you are equipped with the staple ingredients in your kitchen, preparing Korean dishes is actually quite simple and easy. However, the most common ingredients are soy- and/or rice-based, and you'll also find that many premade store-bought sauces are filled with wheat and MSG. To avoid these common allergens but still fully enjoy delicious Korean cooking, I created 100 percent gluten- and grain-free versions of the most commonly used condiments without sacrificing their authentic flavors. You'll find that many dishes in this book include these ingredients, so don't be afraid to scale up on these recipes if you are planning to make Korean cuisine a regular rotation in your home!

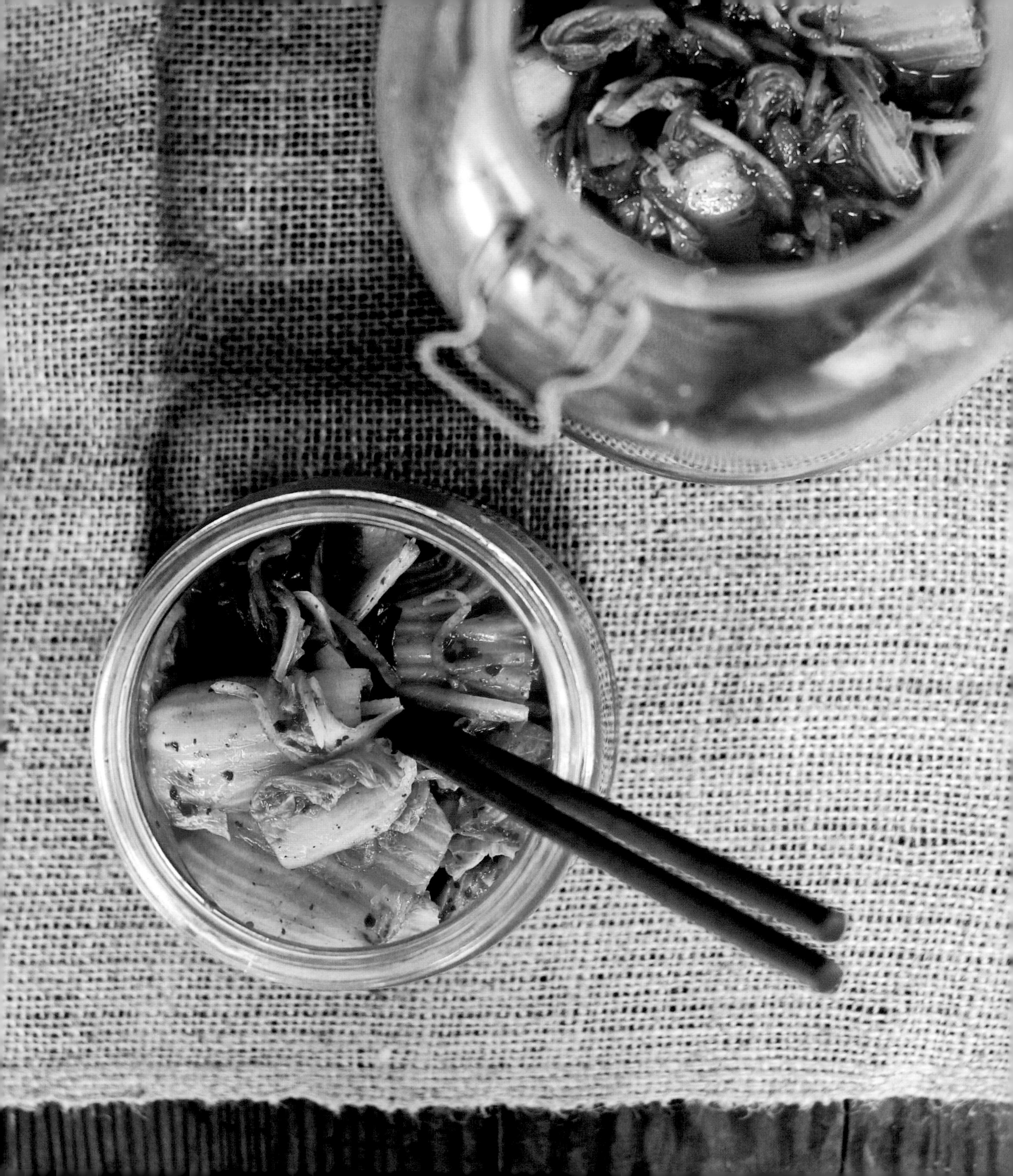

MAK KIMCHI
(Quick Kimchi)

There's something amazingly addictive about this salty, spicy and tangy combo. Although kimchi is technically considered the most famous banchan of all, I decided to list it under this chapter because it's used as an ingredient for so many dishes, and it's definitely a must have for any Korean cooking. Although traditional kimchi making can be a time consuming all-day process, this Mak Kimchi ("mak" literally translates to "careless" or "haphazard") is easy and quick, without sacrificing flavor!

Yields about 16 cups (5.4 kg)

4 lbs (1.7 kg) napa cabbage (about 1 large cabbage)

½ cup (121 g) sea salt

Filtered water

1 lb (454 g) Korean or daikon radish, peeled and julienned

4 green onions, chopped

½ cup (64 g) gochugaru

2 tbsp (30 ml) fish sauce

2 tbsp (36 g) saewoojeot, or substitute with more fish sauce

4 cloves garlic, minced

1" (2.5-cm) piece ginger, minced

1 tbsp (12.5 g) coconut sugar, optional

½ cup (120 ml) water

Wash the outer layers of the cabbage and quarter the heads lengthwise. Remove the core and cut each quarter crosswise into 2-inch (5-cm) pieces. Place the cabbage slices in a large container big enough to fit them, or use 2 smaller containers and divide them evenly.

Sprinkle the salt over the cabbage and massage it into the leaves. Fill up the container with filtered water just until all the cabbage slices are covered. Let soak for 2 hours, stirring the leaves every 30 minutes, until the cabbage leaves are soft and easily bendable without breaking.

Drain the leaves and rinse them thoroughly in cold water, and place them back in the bowl. Add the radish and green onions.

In a separate bowl, combine the gochugaru, fish sauce, saewoojeot, garlic, ginger and coconut sugar, if using. Add ½ cup (120 ml) of water to this mixture and stir well. Pour this over the vegetables in the large bowl. Mix and massage the mixture with your hands so all the vegetables are evenly covered.

Taste the kimchi to decide if you need to adjust the spices. Add more gochugaru for more spicy, fish sauce for more salty and coconut sugar for more sweet. Keep in mind that the spicy and salty flavors will get stronger, while the sweetness will lessen as the kimchi ferments.

Transfer to a 4-quart (4-L) glass jar or a glass container large enough to hold the kimchi. If you don't have a large jar, you can use several smaller ones. Make sure to pack the kimchi tightly into the jar by pressing down with your hand. Leave about 2 inches (5 cm) space at the top before closing the lid.

Let the jar sit out at room temperature out of sunlight for 1 to 2 days until fermented and bubbly and the kimchi has a strong smell. As more liquid forms as it ferments, push down on the kimchi with a spoon so the leaves are mostly submerged under the liquid. Make sure to unscrew the lid every 12 hours during the entire fermentation process to release air bubbles and taste as you go. The kimchi will get more sour and tangier as it ferments.

If you want the kimchi to ferment more, let it sit out longer and taste after 24 hours. Once fermented to your liking, it is ready to eat and you can transfer it into the refrigerator and store it there indefinitely. The kimchi will continue to ferment but at a much slower rate.

Tip: When mixing the spicy sauce with the kimchi vegetables, I highly recommend you wear plastic kitchen gloves. The flavors are extremely strong and may leave your hands tingly and scented with the smell.

GOCHUJANG
(Korean Red Chili Paste)

Gochujang is one of the staple condiments that is present in every Korean household. It's used in a variety of recipes like side dishes, meat marinades and stews, and a little goes a long way because of its strong flavor. This grain-free version tastes just like the real thing and gives a ton of flavor to your dish. Make sure to use fine gochugaru (not coarse flakes) for this recipe!

Yields about 3 cups (720 ml)

1¾ cups (420 ml) water

¼ cup (30 g) tapioca starch

½ tsp honey

2 tbsp (30 ml) molasses

1½ cups (192 g) fine gochugaru

¼ cup (60 g) sea salt

2 tbsp (30 ml) apple cider vinegar or coconut vinegar

In a medium saucepan over medium-high heat, mix together the water and tapioca starch.

Whisk frequently as the mixture heats up. The mixture will turn into a thick paste as it heats.

Once it starts boiling, reduce the heat to low and simmer. Add the honey and molasses and whisk together to avoid clumps. Let this simmer for 20 minutes uncovered, whisking every 5 minutes to avoid burning the bottom. The mixture should thicken and reduce. Turn off the heat and cool until it reaches room temperature, about 30 minutes to 1 hour.

Add the gochugaru, sea salt and vinegar, and whisk together until there are no lumps and everything is incorporated well. If the Gochujang is too thick, add more vinegar, a tablespoon (15 ml) at a time, until it reaches the right consistency. Transfer to a clean glass container.

You can use this Gochujang right away or let it sit out, covered, at room temperature for 2 to 3 days to let it ferment. Open the lid every 12 hours to let it "burp" as it ferments. You can store it in the refrigerator indefinitely. It will slowly ferment the longer it sits, and build more flavor.

PALEO DOENJANG
(Korean Miso Paste)

Doenjang is a Korean version of fermented miso paste that's used almost as much as Gochujang. While no attempt I make will match up to my paternal grandmother's, who has unfortunately passed away without sharing her famous recipe, this grain-free version comes close to the real thing and tastes delicious in recipes like Doenjang Jjigae (Miso Paste Stew) (page 59) and Doenjang Gui (Doenjang Marinated Meat) (page 35).

Yields about 3 cups (720 ml)

1 cup (125 g) cashews

1 cup (130 g) almonds

6 tbsp (90 ml) fish sauce

3 tbsp (45 ml) coconut aminos

2 tbsp (30 ml) apple cider vinegar

2 tsp (12 g) sea salt

2 tsp (12 g) tahini

2 tsp (5 g) fine gochugaru

2 tsp (5 g) onion powder

Soak the cashews and almonds in water for 4 hours to overnight. Drain them, and place them in the food processor with the fish sauce, coconut aminos, vinegar, sea salt, tahini, gochugaru and onion powder. Blend until smooth and creamy, but stop before the mixture turns to a drippy nut butter texture.

Transfer to a clean glass container with an airtight lid. You can use the Paleo Doenjang right away, or close the lid and let it sit at room temperature for a week. Transfer to the refrigerator. The Paleo Doenjang will last for up to 2 weeks.

UMMA'S SSAMJANG

(Dipping Sauce)

Ssamjang is one of those condiments that can be vastly different from one household to another. It's a dipping sauce that can be used for anything you want really, from fresh vegetables to meats, before folding them into a lettuce wrap. I, of course, think that my umma's (mom's) is the best one out there!

Yields about 1 cup (240 ml)

½ cup (138 g) Paleo Doenjang (Korean Miso Paste) (page 177)

½ cup (55 g) walnuts

2 tbsp (30 ml) Gochujang (Korean Red Chili Paste) (page 174)

1 tbsp (15 ml) sesame oil

2 tsp (10 ml) maple syrup, or more to taste

2 cloves garlic

Place the Paleo Doenjang, walnuts, Gochujang, sesame oil, maple syrup and garlic in a blender, and blend until smooth. If the sauce is too spicy, stir in a bit more maple syrup. Serve with your favorite BBQ meats or raw veggies!

HEMP TOFU

While tofu is usually made with soybeans, this version uses hemp seeds to make it Paleo-friendly. You can purchase nigari flakes, a coagulant for the tofu, online or at a Japanese grocery store You can also easily find a plastic tofu mold and cheesecloth online for quite cheap. It's worth making just to cook up a batch of Dubu Buchim (Pan-Fried Tofu with "Soy" Garlic Sauce) (page 110)!

Yields 1 large block of tofu

3 cups (480 g) raw and shelled hemp seeds

8 cups (2 L) water, divided

2 tsp (10 g) nigari flakes

Before you begin, you'll need a tofu mold and a cheesecloth for this recipe.

Working in batches if needed, place the hemp seeds in a high-powered blender with 7 cups (1.7 L) of water. Blend well until smooth and creamy. Strain the liquid through a cheesecloth or a nut milk bag into a large saucepan. Use your hands to squeeze out as much liquid as possible.

Heat the hemp milk on the stovetop over medium-high heat. Let it come to a boil, then turn down the heat to low and let it simmer for 10 minutes. Stir frequently to prevent the milk from burning. You should see the milk curdle and separate.

Remove from the heat and let the curdled milk sit for 7 to 10 minutes until the temperature reaches 165°F (74°C). Measure with a cooking thermometer to get an accurate reading.

Stir the nigari flakes in 1 cup (240 ml) of warm water until dissolved, then add this mixture to the saucepan. Stir 2 to 3 times without over-mixing, then let sit for 30 minutes.

Line the tofu mold with a cheesecloth and place it in the sink. Ladle the hemp milk curds into the mold using a small mesh strainer, and let it drain. Wrap the cheesecloth over the curds and put on the lid of the tofu mold, pressing down gently to squeeze out the liquid.

Place the entire tofu mold in a bowl and transfer it to the refrigerator. Place a heavy object over the lid and let sit for 2 hours in the fridge so the liquid drains out more and the tofu is formed.

Discard the drained liquid and carefully open the cheesecloth to lift the tofu from the mold. You can use the hemp tofu right away or store it submerged in water in the refrigerator. If you do store it, change the water every 24 hours and eat it within 3 days.

> Note: Every nigari is different so you may adjust the amount depending on its formulation and strength. This recipe uses nigari flakes from Raw Rutes.

CAULIFLOWER STICKY RICE

Did you really have a Korean meal if you didn't eat any rice? Since many dishes are spicy and salty, a bowl of sticky rice is always present to balance out the flavors. You'll rarely see non-sticky rice at a Korean table, but feel free to leave out the tapioca starch if you don't love the "stickiness."

Serves 4

1 medium head cauliflower

1 tbsp (15 ml) cooking oil

2 tbsp (30 ml) full-fat coconut milk

2 tbsp (30 ml) apple cider vinegar or coconut vinegar

2 tbsp (15 g) tapioca starch (omit if you want non-sticky rice)

Remove the leaves from the cauliflower and cut off the florets from the roots. Use a cheese grater or a food processor with a grater attachment, and grate the cauliflower into the size of rice.

Heat the cooking oil in a large skillet over medium heat. Add the cauliflower rice and saute until soft and slightly translucent but not mushy, about 5 to 7 minutes.

Take off the heat and immediately add the coconut milk, vinegar and tapioca starch. Stir well and serve.

Note: If you use pre-riced cauliflower, use about 4 cups. Fresh cauliflower rice will work better than the pre-frozen kind.

SWEET AND SOUR DIPPING SAUCE

This all-purpose sauce is a great way to elevate the flavors of dumplings and savory pancakes. The sweet, sour and salty combo is certainly an addictive one, and I remember eating dumplings and making a slit in the wrappers with my chopsticks, so I could spoon this sauce into it to enjoy the flavors in one bite. Try it. It's the best!

Yields about ⅓ cup (80 ml)

2 tbsp (30 ml) coconut aminos

2 tbsp (30 ml) apple cider vinegar or coconut vinegar

1 tbsp (15 ml) water

½ tsp honey

1 green onion, chopped

1 clove garlic, minced

½ tsp sesame oil

½ tsp gochugaru

Stir together the coconut aminos, vinegar, water, honey, green onion, garlic, sesame oil and gochugaru in a small bowl. Serve with your favorite savory pancakes or dumpling.

*See photo on page 171.

STOCKING UP YOUR KOREAN PALEO KITCHEN

While cooking the recipes in this book, you may see ingredients that are new to you and that you've never heard of before. Here's a quick guide to help you navigate some of the most common ingredients used in Korean cooking.

CONDIMENTS

Apple cider vinegar or coconut vinegar

These are the two vinegars that I recommend in Asian cooking in general. Most of the time, Koreans use rice vinegar which is quite harmless; I know that many Paleo eaters still include it in their diets, as do I sometimes. But for those who don't, apple cider vinegar and coconut vinegar seem to most closely resemble the slightly sweet taste of rice vinegar. For apple cider vinegar, I highly recommend the raw and organic kind "with the mother" for its full probiotic benefits.

Coconut aminos

Coconut aminos is a great substitute for soy sauce, which is commonly used in Korean cooking. It's made from the sap of the coconut instead of soy and has a slightly lighter and sweeter taste than soy sauce, while being grain-free and gluten-free. It's quite easy to find at a local health food store these days, making it an essential part of overall Paleo cooking.

Coconut sugar

When it comes to sweeteners, Koreans like to use white sugar and rice syrup. For an all-purpose Paleo sweetener, I've found that coconut sugar works best without being overpowered by any kind of specific taste and compromising the texture of the dish. I also use maple syrup, honey and molasses in several of the recipes as well, but you'll see that coconut sugar appears the most because of its mild, versatile flavor.

Doenjang

This Korean version of soybean paste is different from miso in that it's not fermented with any grains. A true, authentic doenjang only needs soybeans and salt to make, but it's extremely difficult to find one that clean because the process is quite labor intensive. Doenjang is thicker and coarser in texture than miso, and has a pungent cheesy scent from the fermentation. You can find my grain-free recipe in this book, but Wholly, the same company that makes my favorite Gochujang, also makes a great doenjang as well with just three ingredients: soybeans, salt and water. I highly recommend it if you are okay with consuming fermented soybeans.

Fish sauce

With a true umami flavor, fish sauce is used to salt food in various dishes. It's also delicious in kimchi making and actually helps with the fermentation process. High-quality fish sauce is made with some kind of fish and salt that's been fermented for over a year, with no other ingredients or fillers. The only brand I recommend is Red Boat, which is a Vietnamese fish sauce with an amazing flavor.

Gochugaru

These Korean red pepper flakes are used widely in Korean cooking. Since there's almost always at least a bit of spiciness in every dish, you'll find gochugaru in most recipes. There are two types of gochugaru: coarse and fine. The coarse flakes are more commonly used in everyday cooking. The fine powder form is used to make Gochujang (Korean Red Chili Paste) (page 174). I found that the best way to keep gochugaru is to store it in an airtight resealable bag in the freezer.

Gochujang

Gochujang is a thick and sticky red chili paste that's used in marinades, soups and stews, sauces and more. It is typically made with gochugaru, glutinous rice and some kind of sweetener. You can find a delicious Paleo version in this book (page 174), but if you are okay with consuming grains and you want to purchase it instead, make sure there's no wheat or corn syrup in the ingredients list. One of the cleanest brands I found is called Wholly, which you can find online.

Saewoojeot

This one might take a bit more getting used to than others, but it's one of those ingredients you'll love in your cooking once you start using it. Saewoojeot is tiny shrimp that's been salted and fermented, and is commonly used to salt food in Korean cooking. Clean versions are usually easy to find at Asian grocery stores, with just shrimp and salt as the ingredients. If you have a difficult time finding it or you just can't get on board with the concept, you can simply substitute with the same amount of fish sauce.

PRODUCE

Cheongyang peppers

Cheongyang peppers are one of the spiciest peppers in Korea and are used to flavor various dishes. A little goes a long way because of the heat. You can always substitute with jalapeño peppers or serrano peppers in recipes if you have trouble finding cheongyang peppers. Feel free to omit them altogether if you prefer a less spicy dish.

Korean pear

Korean pear, or *bae*, is large and round with a brownish yellow skin. The texture is quite different from a regular pear, and it's more crispy and crunchy like an apple. It's sweet and tart and really delicious. Koreans like to use this pear to sweeten sauces instead of using sugar. Since it's mostly used in cooking to flavor the food with its sweetness in this book, you can substitute with a regular pear or an apple when it's used ground up in recipes.

Korean radish

Moo, or *mu*, is the term for Korean radish. It's different from your typical radish in that it has a white skin with a bit of a green tint on one side, and it's much larger and rounder. It's one of the most common vegetables in Korean cooking, and you'll find it served raw, cooked, fermented and blended into sauces. If you have a hard time finding Korean radish, you can substitute it with daikon radish, which is more common and has a very similar taste and texture.

Mung bean sprouts

While not entirely Paleo, mung bean sprouts are a great, healthy substitute for soybean sprouts, which are commonly used in Korean cooking. I really don't like to use soybeans at all unless they're truly fermented, because of their estrogen-mimicking tendencies that can alter our hormones. Beans and legumes are avoided on the Paleo diet because they contain an anti-nutrient called phytic acid, which binds to beneficial minerals in our body so they aren't available for us to absorb. The sprouting process reduces this effect, making sprouted grains much more easily digestible. If you don't experience any negative symptoms after consuming mung bean sprouts, I wouldn't worry about eliminating them from your diet.

Napa cabbage

This Asian cabbage is the main ingredient in kimchi and can also be used to make lettuce wraps, like Bossam (Pork Belly Wraps) (page 47). It's called *baechu* in Korean, and it has much thicker and tougher leaves than a regular cabbage. They are easy to find at Asian grocery stores, and I've even been seeing them more and more at regular grocery stores as well.

OTHER INGREDIENTS

Cooking oil

I decided not to specify what oils to use for regular cooking like stir-frying and baking, because every Paleo household has its preference of cooking oil no matter what the recipe says. Some great high-heat cooking oils I recommend are coconut oil, avocado oil, ghee, grass-fed butter, lard, tallow, duck fat and other animal fats. I would definitely avoid canola oil, soybean oil, corn oil and other vegetable oils that are often used in Korean cooking. These oils are mostly already rancid when you buy them and contribute to so many diseases and inflammations in the modern world.

Deep-frying oil

There are several deep-fried recipes in this book, and the type of oil you use for them is important because deep-frying is done at a very high temperature. Many oils do not have a high enough smoke point to handle that kind of heat, so it's important to choose ones that are stable enough to withstand the process. Lard, tallow, duck fat, avocado oil, refined coconut oil and palm shortening (from a sustainable source) are all great options to use, but I wouldn't use animal fats for dessert recipes because they can flavor the final dish.

Dried anchovies

Dried anchovies, or *myeolchi*, come in various sizes. To cook from this book, you'll just need the large dried anchovies, which are used to make delicious stock for various soups and stews. They really add so much flavor to the stock when simmered together for a long time. You can find them at Asian grocery stores or order them online.

Dried kelp

Also called *dashima* or *kombu* (in Japanese), dried kelp come in thick, large sheets about 12 inches (30 cm) long and 6 inches (15 cm) wide, but the sizes can vary. They are often cooked with dried anchovies to make flavorful stock, or you can also make a delicious sweet and salty snack with them called TwiGak (Sweet Fried Kelp Chips) (page 167).

Dried seaweed

When I say "dried seaweed" in this book, I'm talking about *mareun miyeok* or *wakame* (in Japanese). It's different from kelp in that it's another type of seaweed that's more stringy and thinner. It comes shriveled up in small pieces that expand in size once they are soaked in liquid. You've probably seen them floating around in miso soup, and in Korean cooking, they are used in recipes like Miyeok Guk (Seaweed Soup) (page 67) and Miyeok Muchim (Seaweed Salad) (page 122).

Dry unseasoned seaweed sheets

You may be confused about how these are different from the previous ingredient. These seaweed sheets are processed completely differently from just dried seaweed. Also called, *gim* or *nori* (in Japanese), these are pulped seaweed that's been dried in a paper-thin layer, then cut into squares. You've probably seen or tried out mini rectangles of roasted seaweed snacks, called Gim Gui (Roasted Seaweed) (page 129) in Korean, and *gim* is what they are made out of. These are also cut into thin strips to flavor and garnish soups and rice bowls.

Kimchi

It wouldn't be Korean cooking without some healthy, probiotic-rich kimchi. It's gotten so popular in the past several years that it really needs no introduction. You can easily make it at home using my Mak Kimchi (Quick Kimchi) recipe (page 173) or you can purchase it at your local health food or Asian grocery store. To keep it Paleo, make sure the store-bought versions do not contain any kind of flour, which is often used to thicken the kimchi sauce.

Nigari

You'll need this ingredient to make Hemp Tofu (page 181), and it is used to firm up and solidify the tofu. It can come in liquid, powder or flake form, but I found that the flakes work best. Nigari is essentially magnesium chloride made by evaporating seawater, which is why it resembles sea salt. There are various qualities of nigari, but the one I like best is the Raw Rutes brand.

Protein

While all meats and seafood get a green light on the Paleo diet, focusing on quality is crucial for the environment, as well as for their nutritional profile. If you can, choose grass-fed and/or pasture-raised animals, preferably from your local farmer. If you can't find sustainable farms or farmers' markets near you, many grocery stores now have grass-fed meats as they have gotten more mainstream. For seafood, wild-caught is preferable over farm-raised, and try to find fish that have been harvested in sustainable ways.

There are actually many companies that deliver high-quality proteins directly to your home, so doing a bit of research to find the best way to source your meats and seafood is worth the positive impacts you'll have on our planet and your health. Of course, don't stress out too much if you have limitations on access and finances. Just do the best you can to provide the highest quality meal that's within your budget and availability.

Sesame

When Koreans use sesame seeds and oil in cooking, which is all the time, it's the toasted version, which has a strong and delicious nutty aroma and taste. When it comes to the oil, I don't specify whether to use the toasted or untoasted kind in the recipes, because it's your preference whether you want the deep, intense flavor of toasted or the lighter taste of untoasted sesame oil.

There's a debate on whether sesame seeds and oil are Paleo or not, because, like vegetable oils, they contain high amounts of omega-6 fatty acids and polyunsaturated fatty acids (PUFAs), which make them sensitive to light, heat and air. PUFAs in oils can make them go rancid easily and cause inflammation in the body. Unlike vegetable and other seed oils, however, sesame seeds are rich in antioxidants, which actually protect the fat in the oil from oxidizing easily, making them quite stable.

Sesame seeds and oil can be harmless in moderation. When choosing sesame oil, I suggest buying one that's un-refined, organic and cold pressed, and comes in a dark, amber bottle so it can be protected from light. I wouldn't use them to cook food in because they are still sensitive to high heat, so add them to your dish at the end for flavoring before serving. Store them in the refrigerator to prolong their stability and flavor.

ACKNOWLEDGMENTS

Gomapseumnida. (Thank you)

To my husband, Charlie, you are my biggest believer and cheerleader, and this book would not be possible without your ongoing support. Thank you for always making me laugh at my most difficult times during the book writing process. I'm the luckiest girl to have met a man who might love Korean food even more than I do.

To my umma, who's always believed that I can do whatever I put my heart into and truly supported me in all my endeavors. You're my best friend. Thank you for being so open-minded about everything I do and shaping me into the strong, hard-working woman I am today.

To my appa, who is my biggest support system. You may not always understand what I do, but I know you want the best for me and I can always count on you to be there no matter what I'm going through. Thank you for being the best dad a girl could ask for.

To YoungJae, my oppa, the artistic one in the family. Thank you for being my biggest inspiration for creativity since childhood. I probably wouldn't have an eye for colors and photography without your influence.

To Munhwachon halmuhnee, my sweet grandma, thank you for raising us while our parents worked full-time and feeding us the most delicious foods without measuring a single ingredient in your life. I only hope my recipes are as half as amazing as your cooking.

To Godok halmuhnee, my other grandma. I wish you were here to see the adult I've become. I know you would be so shocked and proud to see that this little kid, who used to make your life miserable at times with my stubbornness and nonstop crying, wrote a freakin' cookbook.

To Radley and Sally, my two most adorable fur babies. Thank you for licking the floor clean as I cook and make a mess and always being able to put a smile on my face no matter how bad of a day I'm having.

To my readers and followers, I wouldn't have been able to write this book without your love and support. Thank you so much for your enthusiasm and encouraging words during the writing process. What was probably just a nice, small compliment to you has meant the world to me.

Lastly, to the Page Street Publishing team, thank you for making my dream book happen and believing in me. The day you approached this small-time blogger about writing a cookbook may have been one of the most exciting moments of my life.

ABOUT THE AUTHOR

Jean Choi is a Nutritional Therapy Practitioner and the voice behind the real food recipe blog whatgreatgrandmaate.com. When she's not cooking, photographing or concocting natural home remedies, you'll find her cuddling with her two dogs or spending her time outdoors hiking or lounging on a beach near her home in Southern California.

Jean's passion for holistic health started after suffering half of her life with IBS and digestive issues, without being able to find a doctor who could pinpoint exactly what was wrong with her nor alleviate her symptoms without medication. What she thought was her new normal all changed when, through her own independent research, she found out that foods like gluten, dairy and processed sugars were compromising her gut health and making her feel tired and bloated all the time.

She began her Paleo journey in 2012, and fueled by her ability to feel amazing with real food, she decided to become a Nutritional Therapy Practitioner to better understand the body's incredible ability to heal itself when given the right tools. She started What Great Grandma Ate in 2014 to share her experience and the foods that she was eating, hoping she could help and inspire others going through a similar journey as hers.

Today, Jean is a strong believer that the food you love should love you back. It should nourish you while being delicious, and it should be prepared with love and care from quality ingredients. Her biggest passion is to help others discover that healthy home cooking can be fun and easy, and her simple, delicious recipes are a reflection of that.

INDEX